STRAY

A Shelter Veterinarian's Reflection on Triumph and Tragedy

By Dena Mangiamele, DVM, MPVM, MFS

Sale of this book without a front cover may be unauthorized. If this book is coverless, it may have been reported to the publisher as "unsold or destroyed," and neither the author nor the publisher may have received payment for it.

Stray is an autobiographical work. Names, places, and incidents are based on the author's recollection, but they may be fictionalized in some instances to preserve anonimity and respect people's privacy.

Copyright © 2016 Dena Mangiamele. All rights reserved.
This book is not to be copied or reproduced by any means, in whole or in part, without permission from Dena Mangiamele.

The book cover was designed by erowe design.
erowedesign.com

Regarding the illustrations in Chapters 2, 6, 7, 10, and 11: Copyright © 2002-2016 Dena Mangiamele. All rights reserved. These illustrations are not to be copied or reproduced by any means, in whole or in part, without permission from Dena Mangiamele.

Regarding photographs and newspaper articles used in this book: See Chapter 12 for attribution and permissions associated with photographs and newspaper articles.

This trade paperback edition was published in the United States of America.

Praise for *Stray: A Shelter Veterinarian's Reflection on Triumph and Tragedy*:

Stray provides an open and honest look at the reality of pet overpopulation and exploitation and calls all of us who care about animals to support responsible pet ownership and champion our local animal control and shelter professionals. These stories will delight like James Herriot and horrify like Stephen King... a truly important book.
 —Joan Schrader, DVM

The road to progress is always bumpy, especially for those who must convince others that the old way of doing business has been replaced with new and better ways. Change is as hard as it is necessary. Enter the optimist, the one blinded by the desire to bring on change, even when it means being challenged and even discounted. And so begin the trials, tragedy, and triumphs of one Dena Mangiamele, a passionate veterinarian whose love of all things animal comes before her ego. Come along on her journey, from wide-eyed adolescent to a wiser adult. Still the dreamer, still believing that man's dominance over animals is a sacred obligation... Dena's mentors will inspire you too, from the old-fashioned Dr. Perry, to a superstar crusader named Gretchen. The book will make you laugh and cry. It will inspire you to get in the humane arena and cheer for the animals who have put so much trust in us humans.
 —Patricia Dibsie, Director, LOVE HEELS Canine Partners

Dedication

This book is dedicated to my mom who recognized my desire to become a veterinarian when I was a young child. She allowed me to have a variety of animal species throughout my childhood and encouraged my work at a veterinary hospital through my teen years. She used to throw my running shoes at me when she knew I needed a study break as an undergraduate, she understood the challenges of earning a seat in veterinary school, and she supported my decisions as I struggled to find my calling in a veterinary career. I can remember her sewing my Los Angeles City Animal Control veterinary patches onto my uniform shirt sleeves. She looked up at me and said, "You are so proud to be wearing this uniform, aren't you?" She knew all along that shelter work would be the place for me. She just wanted to make sure I was aware that this was my calling. My response was, "I have found it."

Dr. Dena and her mom.

Acknowledgements

I want to thank first and foremost the staff at Los Angeles City Department of Animal Control, especially the Registered Veterinary Technicians, Animal Care Technician Supervisors, and Animal Care Technicians at all six shelters. They trained me, they trusted me, and they taught me the importance of the animal care work that these agencies do on a daily basis throughout the country. To be a part of this family is an honor.

There were so many people that helped guide me and in some cases protect me during my tenure in Los Angeles.

- Peter Persic, our department's public relations director, cultivated the KTLA Morning News Pet of the Week Segment and handled all media requests, which was a major contributing factor to the positive light we had shining on us.
- Jerry Greenwalt was the Assistant General Manager and the best boss I ever had. He let me do my job, never interfered, and was always present for support and direction when I needed it.
- Captain Richard Felosky took the time to share with me his knowledge of running an efficient animal shelter and the importance of supporting and promoting professionalism in his staff.
- Phyllis Daugherty was a tireless animal activist that rescued strays off the streets. She fought for the rights of the animals and the staff, as well as policies to move animal control forward.
- Dan Morrison, Director of South Eastern Animal Control Authority, took me under his wing and was my check and balance man. His kindness and overall knowledge of animal sheltering was something I would always strive to achieve.
- Eric Sakach with the Humane Society of the United States was ever present with every dog- and cock-fighting case we prosecuted, contributing his experience, expertise, and friendship.

- ☐ Marvin Mackie, DVM, was the early-age spay/neuter guru. He unselfishly shared his surgical techniques with fellow professionals and performed more surgeries than one can imagine, all with the goal of lowering pet overpopulation. His commitment to quality lives for animals and his support of animal control and the rescue community are unmatched.
- ☐ Peter Weinstein, DVM, Executive Director of the Southern California Veterinary Medical Association, supported our early-age spay/neuter program. The positive support he generated for our shelters through the professional community was priceless.

It is true it takes a community to raise a child. It also takes a community to protect and care for our stray and abandoned animals. As you can see from all of the varied support I had throughout my journey, I never could have made it on my own. Thank you to each and every one of you. Together, we made it a better place for the animals of Los Angeles in the late 1990's and today.

Dr. Marvin Mackie, Early Age Spay/Neuter Guru, with Dr. Dena.

Table of Contents

Introduction: Why This Book...	1
Forward: Six Locations and 80,000 Animals	7
Chapter 1: East Valley Shelter, Van Nuys, CA	15
Chapter 2: South Los Angeles Shelter, LA, CA	39
Chapter 3: West Valley Shelter, Chatsworth, CA	57
Chapter 4: North Central Shelter, LA, CA	73
Chapter 5: West Los Angeles Shelter, LA, CA	101
Chapter 6: Harbor Shelter, San Pedro, CA	119
Chapter 7: Animal Hoarders and Collectors	139
Chapter 8: Animal Rescue Groups	165
Chapter 9: Dog Exploitation and Dog Fighting	177
Chapter 10: Pal the Pug	187
Chapter 11: Tying Loose Ends Together	199
Chapter 12: Photo Memories	211

Dr. Dena sketched this dog trapped by rising flood waters during Hurricane Katrina. Animal Control employees rescue animals in all kinds of situations, including natural disasters.

Introduction:
Why This Book...

We all have experiences throughout our lives that we revisit through memories. As time lengthens between the actual events and the memory, details may be lost and lessons learned forgotten. I put this memoir together to ensure that my experiences as an animal shelter veterinarian could be used by individuals considering a career in shelter medicine, those that are actively engaged in shelter work, and those that support or question the work it takes to honorably operate an animal control sheltering facility.

This is not a technical manual on shelter operations but my true life experiences that, at one end of the spectrum, stole my heart, and at the other end of the spectrum, left me to this day saddened and unconsolable. With the help of my devoted staff, who make up the colorful characters in this book, and the thousands of animals we cared for daily, I am able to tell my story.

I found my way to the animal shelter based on one thing—my love for animals. I stayed despite the heartache, frustration, misunderstandings, and exhaustion because there was still so much more work to do to make this world a better place for our animal companions.

Despite the fact that, as an animal control agency, we rescued homeless, sick, and injured animals from the streets, the reality was that there were only three ways for an animal to leave the shelter: reuniting lost pets with their owners, adopting-out animals, or humane euthanasia. All options were directly or indirectly controlled by space constraints or financial shortcomings, both of which we had in abundance. The constant flow of unwanted and disposable animals resulted in high daily euthanasia numbers. For all of us who worked at animal control for the sole reason that we wanted to help animals, this black curtain of death was our darkest hour. We reconciled ourselves to our post traumatic stress by working to address the underlying causes of pet overpopulation—irresponsible pet owners and individuals that exploited animals.

Our critics were heavy-handed and often times brutal in their attacks. Many did not understand that we were not a humane society and that these two institutions had different mandates. Once they truly understood the differences, it laid the foundation for improved relationships with the public and the rescue community, creating greater respect and compassion for the shelter staff.

The first six chapters of this memoir are dedicated to each of the six animal control shelters in the City of Los Angeles, Department of Animal Control. Some of the stories were painful for me to write and will be painful for you to read. But for you to understand the plight of the animals and those that care for them, there must be an accurate and true accounting of what happens at an animal shelter. As you turn the last page of this book, I hope you join our team and support your local animal control agency, becoming a part of the solution to help care for the lost and unwanted animals in your community.

How It All Started...

As far back as I can remember, all of my Italian relatives would ask me what I wanted to be when I grew up, and my answer was always the same, a veterinarian. In grade school, I knew every dog breed and got my hands on a skeletal diagram of a dog and memorized every bone. By seventh grade, my mom gave me the first James Herriot book for Christmas, *All Creatures Great and Small*. It chronicled the adventures of a country large-animal veterinarian in England, and I was hooked. I went on to read the next two books in the series, and I dreamed of a life caring for animals and at the same time helping people. In eighth grade, everyone in my class participated in the school science fair. I partnered with my best girl friend, and we set up a project with our local mid-west small-animal veterinarian where we injected mice with different drugs and recorded the effects on their heart rates. Although we didn't win the fair, we did get honorable mention, and it gave me the opportunity to be behind the scenes at a veterinary hospital.

Back in the 1970's, most veterinary practices were owned and operated by one doctor who specialized in every aspect of veterinary medicine. Many of them also had additional revenue streams such as dog breeding, grooming services, and boarding kennels. My dad suggested that I call the vet who'd helped me with the science fair project and ask if I could volunteer at the hospital a couple of days a week. He told me that if I worked hard, he was sure I would be offered a job. I thought this was a crazy idea because why would you hire someone if you weren't advertising for a new employee? I finally got up the nerve to call the doctor and ask if I could come by the hospital and volunteer. As it turned out, he was quite pleased to have my free labor, and I was scheduled to come by the following Saturday.

When I arrived, I had an introduction to the day-to-day operations at a veterinary hospital. I received my first assignment prior to the arrival of clients. I was to safely relocate all of the dogs that were boarding at the hospital from the kennel runs to holding cages so I could hose down and squeegee the enclosures from a night's worth of urine and feces. Despite the smell (thirty dogs can make quite a mess in a 12-hour period), I couldn't have been happier, knowing I was making a clean space for them. It took me a while to get "the feel" of the strength of the hose when power washing the kennels, so I came out a bit wet myself, but I didn't mind. I meticulously cleaned each pen, replaced food and water bowls, and opened the windows to facilitate the drying process before I put the dogs back in their kennels. The kennel work was such a blessing in disguise because it gave me a foundation in animal handling that would serve me well later in my career as a shelter veterinarian.

As the morning progressed, clients came in for their scheduled appointments. I assisted the doctor by holding animals on the exam table during office calls while he examined them and administered vaccinations.

Later in the morning, the schedule switched to surgeries. My mom was a registered nurse, and she told me that an important step to finding out if I could really be a veterinarian was to watch a surgical procedure and make sure "I could handle it." I wasn't sure exactly what that meant, so I had no preconceived notions as I entered the surgical suite to watch a spay surgery. I watched as the doctor carefully made the first skin incision on this small mixed-breed dog, and as he carefully dabbed the blood from the site. He explained every step to me, and soon he was in this animal's body cavity and somehow he had located the uterus. I was fascinated, and not until the surgery was over and I was cleaning up the instruments and sanitizing the surgical table did I realize that "Yes, I *could* handle it."

The day continued, and a lot of the work was continual clean up for the animals that were boarding at the hospital, that and sweeping and mopping floors. I didn't mind because I knew it made the animals comfortable and I wanted them to be happy under my care.

When I got home that evening, I wanted that job even more than making cheerleading. (Give me a break—I was fourteen years old!) Two days after volunteering, I got a phone call from Dr. Perry, and I still remember his words to this day. "Well, how would you like to get on the payroll?"

I was so excited and couldn't wait to get back to that hospital. Not until much later did I realize that my dad probably had some influence on setting up my volunteer work and securing that job. Thanks, Dad...

I started the job before I even had a driver's license and continued to work there through college. I have fond memories of colorful characters that were regular clients and their pets. After the first few years, many of the clients would only board their animals at the hospital if they knew I would be there working in the back caring for them, and it made the work even more rewarding.

Some of my favorites were a pair of black Great Danes, Gabby and Walker; a little Boston Terrier that I ended up adopting, Miss T; and the resident hospital cat Benjamin. "Bennie" was an orange tabby with orange eyes. (This combination is the undisputed most-sociable cat you will find.) Not only was he the overall proprietor of the hospital but he was also a media star in his own right. His presence was frequently requested at the photographer's studio down the street to pose for several advertising campaigns. I spoiled him rotten since I was in charge of the cattery and would sneek him special canned food in the evening. I have personally owned two orange tabbies throughout my life, and all have proven to have similar traits to the master, Benjamin.

Bennie's best friend was the doctor's breeding schnauzer bitch, Minnie Pearl. She had a beautiful haircoat of silver and black that was as soft as silk. She arrived every morning with the doctor and went home every evening with him. She was a great tennis ball retriever and was willing to chase the ball down the back corridor for hours and replace it in the desk drawer when we were finished with playtime. She made my daily cleaning chores go by quickly, she was by my side for most of the day, and I loved her. Bennie and Minnie Pearl were icons at that hospital and were often found wrestling in the waiting room. Dr. Perry was like a second father to me, and since he had four sons, I really was his adopted daughter! Even after I had graduated from veterinary college and moved to California, Dr. Perry and his wife would come out West and visit me. We had a bond for life. Dr. Perry is no longer with us, but I hope he knew what a tremendous influence he was on my life as a person and a veterinarian.

Dr. Dena with Dr. Robert Perry (her mentor and dear friend for over 25 years).

The Next Steps in My Career

After graduating from veterinary school, my first veterinary management position was with a national pet food manufacturing company as director of the nutrition and palatability center. After a couple of years, I was restless and looking for greater excitement and challenge in my work. I saw the advertisement for the Chief Veterinarian position with the City of Los Angeles, Department of Animal Control, and took a chance by submitting my application. I soon left the predictability of the nutrition center and entered the world of shelter medicine in 1996. Not only was the field of shelter medicine novel to me, but so was the City of Los Angeles—the place I would soon call home.

Forward:
Six Locations and Eighty Thousand Animals

My career as a shelter veterinarian started in the mid-to-late 1990's when animal sheltering agencies were at the cusp of progress. It would still take years (some agencies would take another decade) to leave behind the old ways of animal care and housing, fully recognize the importance of the human-animal bond, join the technical revolution, and change the method of euthanasia to use of injectable drugs. I wrote this book because I feel it is important to document this time period in animal sheltering because it came before the advanced technology advantages of the Internet. Shelters today have enhanced capability to find lost pets, increased visibility regarding animals housed in shelters nationwide (which leads to increased adoptions), and can educate more people about the importance of spaying/neutering in order to lower euthanasia rates. The world is much different today, and over the past twenty years, animal shelters and the animals are much better off because of it.

Those of us that worked in animal control at this time, under conditions that many today would say are unbelievable and unacceptable, were essentially trail blazers for many common procedures like early age spay/neuter and microchipping for increased owner redemptions of lost pets. We could have stayed in the past, but we chose progress, and I believe we played an important role in animal history. Every animal control shelter, every state, had their own issues and growing pains, and there are many versions of this story to tell. Here is my story of working at one of the largest animal control agencies in the country...

My adventures as Chief Veterinarian with the City of Los Angeles, Department of Animal Control, began in 1996 and lasted four rewarding years. My territory covered 470 square miles and included six animal control shelters. That's right—

the city operated not one, not two, but six very large animal shelters. These facilities brought in (impounded) 80,000 animals per year. Each shelter had its own personality and reflected the people in the surrounding community. In the following chapters, I share with you some of the unique stories and incidents that truly reflected each location.

Two of the challenges were the number of diverse ethnicities and the continual population growth in Los Angeles. There was always someone new to educate about responsible pet ownership, which made it difficult to promote consistent and appropriate animal care for pets throughout the city. From China Town to the high socioeconomic status region of West Los Angeles, there were continual pressures and demands that often times resulted in 12-to-14-hour-long days. The other major obstacle was traffic, which didn't even come close to the level of traffic we see today. The high number of commuters often dictated the time I could spend at a shelter and the number of visits I could make to shelters daily. I always said that there is never a dull moment in Los Angeles—and that is as realistic as it gets. The city itself is fast moving, original, and inspiring. It sets a wonderful backdrop for progressive visions and missions.

My responsibilities encompassed animal care, law enforcement, and regular television appearances to promote responsible animal care in Los Angeles. I provided and supervised animal care at all locations for each animal that entered the shelter system. I had the honor of working with licensed Registered Veterinary Technicians (RVTs), including foreign veterinarians (not yet licensed in the state and working in the capacity of technicians). These folks were truly the backbone of the shelter's medical division, and I shall forever be grateful for their time and patience in training me, as well as their devotion to caring for the animals.

After the first several years, I was given additional supervisory responsibility over the kennel staff. For years, the medical and kennel division had operated separately. We combined them and called our new division Animal Care. This proved to be one of the most beneficial reorganizations for the animals that we could have implemented. It created a positive dialogue between divisions and a team atmosphere that improved morale, quality of animal care, and efficiency of service to the public. In essence, we became a family with secure ties that to this day have not broken.

In the law enforcement arena of animal control, I traveled with field officers on humane investigations, including animal-hoarding and dog- and cock-fighting cases. I became an expert witness in court to testify against the enormously cruel world of dog fighting. I inspected kennels and animal research facilities to monitor compliance with humane animal care and handling, and I enhanced my knowledge of exotics through our program of circus inspections, ensuring compliance with exhibitor regulations for animal care and public health and safety within the city.

Throughout this book, I provide you with only a taste of the multitude of activities (including fond memories as well as tragic events) at one of the busiest animal control agencies in the United States. I share with you experiences that will make you feel proud, overwhelmed with sadness, and hopeful all wrapped into one. My desire is to create a new awareness for those who are callused towards, do not approve of, or are misinformed about the value of daily work at governmentally operated animal control shelters. I hope you enjoy and learn from the journey that I have treasured.

Animal Control Agencies and Humane Societies

Many people think there is only one type of animal shelter. Actually there are two main types: animal control agencies and humane societies. What is the difference between these two? A humane society is a private entity that does not report to the local governing body, while an animal control agency is operated and funded by the local city or county government. Humane societies create their own policies and procedures that govern which animals they accept from the public and bring into their facilities for adoption. Because their existence and operation depends on fund raising and donations, they generally choose to accept animals into their facility that are highly adoptable, including the cutest puppies/kittens and healthy, non-aggressive animals. They reserve the right to turn away an animal, and those unwanted animals are sent down the street to the local animal control agency, which is mandated by law to house every stray animal that is brought to their facility.

- ☐ This is why you will see sick and injured animals at animal control. They don't have the luxury of picking or choosing which animal comes into the facility.

- ☐ This is why you will see a large concentration of pit bulls and pit bull crosses at animal control shelters.

- ☐ This is why you will see much larger numbers of animals housed at animal control and higher euthanasia numbers due to the continual number of stray animals that are presented daily and can't be turned away.

When animal control kennels are filled to capacity and stray animals continue to be dropped off at their door by the public or brought in by animal control officers from street patrols— they must make room for them. In order to create new kennel space openings, animals currently housed there must leave the facility. There are four paths an animal exiting the shelter can take. An animal can be redeemed by its owner, an animal can be adopted/taken by a rescue, an animal can die, and as a last resort, an animal can be euthanized at the facility. If the shelter is filled to capacity (which means exceeding the maximum number of animals allowed per cage or kennel run), and the daily number of adoptions and redemptions is lower than the number of animals brought into the shelter, staff must manage the population with the only option left, which is euthanasia. This is usually not an issue for a humane society since they can manage their animal population by lowering or eliminating daily animal intake until adoptions increase, opening up cage and kennel space.

As you are reading this, you might say animal control should just hold more animals per cage. It has to be better than euthanizing animals... I have worked in some of the busiest animal control shelters in the country, and to minimize euthanasia, we were housing 6-8 dogs per kennel—kennels that were constructed to house one large dog or two medium-sized dogs.

As a shelter veterinarian, I can tell you about the horrific incidents that occur when you overcrowd dogs in this way. Because most animals impounded into an animal control shelter are not spayed or neutered, the males and females must be separated. So each kennel either has all males in it or all females. Consider for a minute how 6-7 intact large male dogs would get along in a small kennel for any length of time. Not only is there fighting, resulting in injury to the dogs, there is food fighting/protection. (The weakest one in the kennel may not be allowed to eat and essentially starves for days on end until he/she is identified as a special-needs dog). During the late evening hours when only one kennel attendant is on duty to monitor over 200 dogs, it is not uncommon to find animals that have been killed by other kennel mates. This is not the answer to lower euthanasia rates in an animal control shelter.

If you house animals in an overcrowded environment, the issue of increased disease transmission also becomes a factor. Many stray animals don't come into animal control shelters showing signs of illness, but they are harboring disease that may break out one or two days after they are impounded. During those first few days when they are not showing clinical signs of disease, they are housed in the main kennel with other dogs, essentially exposing them to disease. Even if an animal has a strong immune system, the overall stress of kennel life is a contributing factor in many animals becoming ill. This becomes a vicious cycle, and it's one of the main reasons you find a higher number of ill animals at animal control versus a humane society. It is very difficult to handle this problem because creating an isolation area for new impounded animals would mean taking away general housing space. This would lower the facilities' overall animal holding capacity, causing an increase in euthanasia rates.

Don't get me wrong. Both humane societies and animal control agencies are needed in communities, and both have a special function. The problem comes when the public starts to compare them without understanding the realities and limits of government funding, mandates to accept every stray animal, and how disease transmission and overpopulation in animal control shelters contributes to higher euthanasia rates. As soon as I understood the differences between the two agencies, I knew that animal control was the agency that needed the most support, and that it would be my career choice for shelter medicine.

So please, support your local animal control shelter. Try to understand what you will be seeing when you visit and why those less-than-ideal circumstances exist for the animals housed there. Also know that the staff are compassionate and chose to work for animal control for the same reasons I did. It's where animals need our help the most.

Definitions and Explanations

Simplified Organizational Chart: City of Los Angeles Department of Animal Control

General Manager
Assistant General Manager

Law Enforcement	Animal Care Division	Chief Veterinarian / Veterinary Medical Division	Administrators
Lieutenants (Shelter Supervisors)	Animal Care Technician (ACT) Supervisors (one at each shelter)	Registered Veterinary Technicians (RVT)	Budget
Animal Control Officers	Animal Care Technicians (ACTs)	Shelter Veterinarians (unfilled for first 3 years of my employment)	Licensing
Shelter Clerical Staff			Permits

Chapter One:
East Valley Shelter, Van Nuys, California

No Valley Girls To Be Found...

It was 7:30 A.M., and in the East Valley, you could already feel the heat of the August day starting to creep under your skin. I pulled off the freeway that didn't seem so bad this morning because it only took 50 minutes to get from my house in Belmont Shore, Long Beach, to the Sherman Way exit in the East Valley. I fell in love with Belmont Shore after living there while working at my past position managing animal care for a national pet food manufacturer. It gave me more of a beach environment and provided a buffer from the fast pace of Los Angeles.

In my government issued Ford celebrity, I rolled down the driver's side window while waiting for the light to change at the end of my freeway exit. The air was thick, unclean, and smelled of fried foods. I hadn't made it a point to notice before, but the sidewalks were scattered with paper, fast food containers, and solicitation flyers. Young girls, posing as mothers, were standing on the sidewalk or pushing their newborn children in baby buggies. The street was lined by industrial, blue-collar businesses. How many auto repair and tire shops were needed in the Valley? The light changed to green, and I made my way onto the busy street.

I was a young woman, thirty-five years old, driving alone in a rough city that was starting to become my home. How could it be that a mid-West girl could feel comfortable covering the 470 square mile territory that comprised the City of Los Angeles? I guess some people plan every step of their career and know exactly where they are going, how they are going to get there, and exactly when they plan to arrive. The only thing I ever knew was that I wanted to be a veterinarian.

I planned accordingly, took the proper undergraduate courses, concentrated on keeping high grades, applied to several veterinary colleges, got accepted, and finished the grueling four-year schedule. Then came the National Boards, the State Boards, and clinical competency tests. Thank goodness I didn't know all of that at the beginning because I am sure it would have been too much even to contemplate as a freshman out of high school. Nevertheless, none of that could have prepared me for my current position as Chief Veterinarian for the City of Los Angeles, Department of Animal Control. This was my first year here, and despite my mid-West background, I thrived on the hustle and bustle of this exciting, yet dangerous, city.

As I continued to make my way down Sherman Way, it was easy to confuse blocks with private businesses stacked one on top of another. I used the doughnut shops as landmarks, counting them until I reached four, and then slowed my car down. I tried to locate the animal shelter driveway, and in anticipation, I put my right turn signal on. It was hard to see the sign for the shelter because it was blocked by a tire store that regularly had customers lined up onto Sherman Way in their dented and non-smog certified cars, anticipating their low cost deals. I really don't even know why we bothered putting the sign out. It was only visible as you passed the driveway, and even if you could see it, you certainly couldn't read the words on the sign. They were obliterated by streaks of spray paint that formed insignias of the local territorial gangs.

I turned into the parking lot and hoped one of the four shaded parking places was still available. Damn, of course they were already taken. I really didn't want to get back into my car in the next couple of hours and burn my fingers on the steering wheel, so I turned into the adjacent driveway that was for "employees only" and drove up to the padlocked gate.

One of the interesting quirks about this job was the number of keys one had to carry in order to be able to actually work at the animal shelter. However, there was one universal, magic key that was used at all six shelters throughout the city, called the "IC-80". Whenever you were in doubt and you faced a locked main gate, door to a room, or a locked cage or kennel, you should always try your IC-80 key to see if you could gain entry. Nine times out of ten, it probably worked. Whenever it didn't turn in a lock, it always made me curious. It would mean an additional expense for the city to call out the locksmith and have a special key made for an individual lock. Then the Supervising Officers had to decide which employees needed copies of the key, adding further expense for distribution and monitoring to make sure that only those who absolutely required access actually had it. You usually could tell the rank of an employee by listening for the jingle of the keys attached to the uniform belt. The tone of the rattling determined the number of the keys—the more keys, the more important the employee.

I strategically parked my car back from the gate. I had to calculate the outward swing of the gate once it was opened so that it didn't swing into the front of my car. The reason unlocking the gate was usually so troublesome was that all of my keys were on my key ring, which was currently attached to the key in my car ignition. So I turned the engine off, removed the keys from the ignition, slid out from behind the wheel, and approached the gate. As is customary in most monetarily deprived, governmentally operated animal control shelters, the buildings and equipment were primitive and falling apart in front of your eyes. The gate was chain link with a separate, long, thick chain interlaced between the movable and stationary portions, and the chain was attached to an IC-80 keyed padlock hanging from its center.

On a good day, that padlock would be facing in the direction from which you wished to enter the gate. Unfortunately, as Murphy's Law dictates, the padlock was usually facing the opposite side of the gate, and it was difficult to maneuver it, stick the key in the bottom, and actually disengage the lock's base from the arm. I was lucky today, for an Animal Control Officer, affectionately called an ACO, must have recently driven out of the gate and locked it behind them because the lock was facing me, and I easily manipulated it, untangled the heavy, dirty chain, and swung the gate open.

I looked down at my hands, and they were now smudged with grime from the chain. I reached down to the side of my city uniform pants and casually brushed the dirt from my fingers and palm. If this was the worse dirt I encountered all day, then I would be lucky. I got back into my car and drove through the gate about ten or twelve feet. I started to get out of my car again to re-secure the premises and close the gate, but I was met by one of the Kennel Attendants who waved me on because they were getting ready to unlock the gates at 8:00 A.M. when the shelter opened to the public. The attendant looked tired, his uniform was dirty, and his pant legs were wet from the constant hosing down of the dog kennels. I recognized him as the graveyard shift worker and knew that he was getting ready to head home because he had been on duty since midnight.

I drove past the administrative/clerical building and parked adjacent to the dog kennel area. For some reason at this shelter in particular, I always had a claustrophobic feeling when I arrived. The entire compound was surrounded by chain link fence with razor wire above it as a constant reminder of the neighborhood and dangers that surrounded us. The properties next to the shelter contained old, dilapidated buildings encompassed in cement and blacktop. The shelter followed the design of the area and was harsh, unfriendly, and constructed of cement throughout. All of the neighboring buildings seemed right on top of each other, but no one knew the proprietors or attempted to get to know them. It all was so overwhelming that, for a brief second, I feared that I would be trapped here, that I would faint and no one would know the difference, that the people working in nearby businesses wouldn't even bother to stop and take notice, let alone provide assistance. You had the feeling that you were on your own, and that you had to fend for yourself. Unfortunately, this feeling also extended to the animals that were housed here because they ended up here because people, their owners, didn't bother to take notice of them or come looking for them.

This was such an unlikely place for a shelter to be located. Who would consciously put animals here? Animals longed for regular human companionship, grass to run on—all of which were absent here. I guess that's why this job became so important to me. It was so easy for the public, the community, to forget about these animals, ignore why they were here, and not even contemplate their limited stay. I naively thought that I could change how it was for these animals, I could convince people to take on the responsibility of their pets, and just because I was dedicated and persistent, it would all fall into place. But I came to understand that I would have to settle for much less. As I look back now, I realize I had so much to learn.

I was the only veterinarian on staff at the time, and the six shelters brought in over 80,000 animals per year. The East Valley shelter was undeniably one of the busiest shelters in the state of California. It would not be uncommon for close to 50 animals to be brought from the surrounding community into a full kennel daily. They arrived for a multitude of reasons. They were running loose on the streets, they were injured, they were dangerous, they had been involved in illegal dog fighting, or their owners just didn't want them anymore because they were too much trouble. That meant that 50 animals had to leave the shelter in order to maintain a healthy and safe shelter environment for the animals, the staff, and the public.

Of the four ways to leave a shelter, the best scenario would be for people to come to the shelter and identify and claim their lost pets. The second best way for an animal to exit the shelter would be to become adopted. Unfortunately, the East Valley shelter was the busiest shelter for taking in animals, not for people to claim their pets, nor for adoptions. That left only two alternatives, natural death and humane euthanasia. The latter was unfortunately, a daily ritual.

The Fourth Exit

As a veterinarian, I had euthanized people's pets in private practice, but this was something so different, so disturbing. Yet everyone involved with the shelter had to find a way to cope with it so that we could continue to care for the other animals in the shelter, provide them with whatever human companionship we could, and hope that their owners would come looking for them.

How do you care for hundreds of animals in one shelter, day after day, knowing that 65-70% will eventually have to be euthanized? How do you not become callused? How do you stay sane?

I will tell you. First of all, it is not easy and not just anyone can do it. It takes a special person, one who cares for animals above and beyond the average person. Many well-meaning yet misdirected so-called "animal zealots" who don't work at shelters cannot come to terms with the shelter employee for the very reason that employees have no choice but to euthanize animals in this environment. These folks can be downright vicious to shelter employees when, actually, the shelter employees are the people they should be thanking for caring for the abandoned and unwanted animals— animals that no one else seems to have the time or desire to care for on a daily basis. The zealot favors quantity of life, rather than quality.

Because shelter employees witness the results of so much cruelty and pain that animals have suffered on the streets, they know that, sometimes, there is only one way either to ensure that the suffering for a particular animal will not continue or to end the suffering, and that is euthanasia. As long as there are overcrowded and non-animal-caring communities, there will be animal shelters, and there will be some degree of euthanasia. This is the reality.

How does a shelter employee come to terms with daily euthanasias? You reach deep down inside yourself and use your mind and your heart to reason it through. You quickly understand that you cannot take 50-60 animals from the shelter to your home every day. You work on trying to get as many of the animals adopted as you can by contacting rescue groups, but they are usually already filled to capacity. All of us do end up taking some of the animals home, and we provide loving homes for these special animals. But you can't take each one of them, so then you must ask yourself this question: "Are these animals that we cannot find a home for better off being euthanized, or should they be released to roam freely, wander the streets, starve, live life without any companionship, face injury (fighting, hit by cars) and illness, and ultimately endure a painful, torturous death?"

A reasonable person would have to say, "No, I cannot allow an animal to suffer in that way. I would rather painlessly and humanely euthanize that animal." Don't try to fool yourself. There is no way a domesticated animal will survive roaming on the streets. Again, it becomes a life of quality, rather than quantity. The short time that shelter employees care for these animals may be the best days of these animals' lives up to that point. If you look closely at them, you will know this is true. Not everyone can understand this, nor do they want to. However, it is the truth all the same.

I parked my car, checked to make sure I was wearing my pager on my belt (that's right—cell phones were large, cumbersome, and very expensive at this time), grabbed my notebook and a pen, and headed out to take a look at the animals. I tried to check in at the administrative building of each shelter first so they'd know I was there, but sometimes the animals sidetracked me. This was one of those days. From where my car was parked, I could easily visualize the outdoor section of half of the dog kennel runs. Each one had at least three to four dogs in them, all pushed up against the exterior of the chain link, anxiously watching and vocalizing about my every move from the car as I approached them.

The noise in a large-sized kennel can be deafening. All staff is now equipped with ear protection, but it wasn't always that way. Some employees have permanent hearing loss or are deaf due to their 15-20 years working in these kennels. It becomes one of the on-site job hazards that many outside folks don't realize shelter employees must endure, physically and mentally. It is kind of like listening to children screaming or crying, all day long.

I am always amazed at the number of purebred dogs that find their way to a kennel. In front of me that day I saw a Rottweiler, an Akita, a Maltese, a Shar Pei, and a Jack Russell Terrier. Many of you may not be aware of the fact that up to 25% of the shelter population is purebred dogs. Of course, the majority is a variety of mixed breed dogs. Some are truly comical with their Basset Hound bodies and German Shepherd heads and erect ears. The increasing numbers of Pit Bull Terriers that are in animal control shelters is also indisputable and troubling.

Pit bulls are walking tanks of strength and endurance. At no fault of their own, mankind has bred these dogs to be aggressive and unforgiving when engaged in a fight. For that reason, they are what we call in a shelter, a "keep alone." That means that they must be housed by themselves and not with other dogs. You can imagine what a hardship this is, to take up an entire kennel for just one dog when kennel space is highly needed. This means that, on a daily basis, other adoptable animals are euthanized in order to continue to hold these animals in the shelter.

In addition, pits are usually a high liability adoption. By that I mean that, in the short period of time that the shelter has contact with an animal, it is very difficult to know everything about each animal's individual temperament and actions. It is well known that most pits (those that find their way to shelters anyway) generally don't get along with other dogs, and their idea of a fight is a fight to the death. They also are very stimulated by small animals such as cats, and even by small breed dogs. This predator-prey relationship can result in death for the small animal. This risk of injury or even death extends to the unknowing public if this animal is adopted and (god forbid) gets away from the owner and runs loose on the street or becomes stimulated to attack.

Now, let's also look at this from the angle of protecting this breed. This breed is the one most commonly used in brutal, backyard and professionally-staged, illegal dog fighting. These animals must also be protected from people who force them to participate in this blood sport. Many backyard dog fighters adopt these dogs from shelters to introduce or reintroduce them into the trade as fighters or use them as sparring dogs. Due to the high degree of loyalty of this breed to their owners, they will do whatever they have to in order to please their owner/trainer. I have seen these dogs continue to fight after their limbs have been crushed and broken by the jaws of their opponent. I have seen these animals after a fight with so much blood loss that their owners have left them to bleed out and die. How can a shelter ensure that, once these animals are adopted from the shelter, they will not be forced to endure such cruelty? Screening adoption applicants in a community like Los Angeles to ensure that they will not be using pit bulls for this purpose becomes almost impossible.

Now, all of you who own pit bulls and say they are great pets, I do understand. Not every pit is out there to seek and destroy, and many are successfully adopted. However, adopting a pit bull from a shelter becomes a multifaceted responsibility. Tragically, during the late 1990's, the situation of pet overpopulation was overwhelming. The staggering number of animals entering animal shelters daily coupled with limited holding space, irresponsible breeding for aggression, and lower adoption rates for pits, ended up being a lethal combination for pit bulls who often faced euthanasia as their final disposition.

On that day, as I continued to walk through the animal holding area, I turned my attention to, not only the animals, but the condition of the kennels. The kennel staff on the graveyard shift had freshly hosed all kennel floors. Water bowls were filled with clean, fresh water, and the feeders were in place in each dog run. I walked around to the indoor portion of the kennels and watched the kennel attendant start to padlock all of the cages once again in anticipation of opening the shelter to the public.

Many people wonder why the shelter is so cold and institutional in appearance, with locks on the animal's cages and high security. The fact of the matter is that, if that weren't done, animals would be stolen from the shelter daily. People still do find ways to steal animals despite all of the kennel security, the razor wire surrounding the shelter, and 24-hour staff on the premises. If your pet was lost and ended up in the shelter, how would you feel if someone stole your pet before you had a chance to come to the shelter and claim it? So in fact, it is the community that has created the high security environment at a shelter.

I did a quick walk through, visualized each animal, and made notes on my pad of my observations and any questions on individual animals I might need to ask the Senior Animal Care Technician (ACT) or the Registered Veterinary Technician (RVT) when I met up with them. I monitoried the individual kennel cards that were affixed to the front of each kennel identifying the animal in the holding space. This card provides information on the day the animal was impounded into the shelter; a description of the breed, gender, and approximate age of the animal; and the animal's assigned impound number. It also identifies if an animal is currently being treated for an injury or illness. The card also documents the date the animal will be available for adoption. Each animal that enters a shelter must be held the legal holding period. This varies from state to state, but generally it's from 3 to 7 days. This allows pet owners time to find their lost pets instead of animals being adopted the same day they enter a shelter.

This does not mean that all animals in shelters are euthanized after the legal holding period. It only means that after this time period, the animal becomes the property of the governmentally operated shelter. The shelter has many options and may put the animal up for adoption while waiting for a qualified adopter. If no member of the public is interested in adopting the animal, the shelter may contact a purebred rescue group to take the animal if it meets the group's qualifications. If the shelter staff feels that the animal is unique, but the right adopter just has not come into the shelter (i.e., the staff have fallen in love with the animal), the animal may be transferred to one of the other City shelters that has a higher adoption rate in hopes that it will be adopted there. Many animals are held weeks and even months past their available dates. However, some that are determined not fit for adoption, ill or injured with conditions that are not improving, or when the kennels become overcrowded, then the decision to euthanize animals can be made once the legal holding period has been completed.

As one can imagine, because public animal shelters are forced to euthanize animals, they may not be particularly popular with animal special interest groups. People who affiliate with these groups range from well-meaning animal advocates to misinformed animal fanatics. For the past twenty years or so, there has been a cycle of frustration, I call it, that has been going around and around when it comes to these people and their response to public animal shelters. These folks sincerely want all animals to live happily in permanent homes, but they just can't figure out why there isn't a good home for every animal in the community.

The result for them is frustration, and the end result for the shelter is that some animals have to be euthanized. When it gets to this point, the animal zealots refuse to think with their minds. They only feel with their hearts and react purely on emotion. The activists begin to target the shelter and its employees as the cause of euthanasia in order to find relief for their frustration. Unfortunately, the true cause of overpopulation is the irresponsible animal owner who allows their animal to breed indiscriminately, contributing to the ever increasing number of unwanted animals in our community.

However, it is much easier to point a finger at a shelter employee rather than take the time to identify individuals in the community who act irresponsibly and try to change their animal care practices. In essence, it is a cop-out by the zealots and a selfish way to find short-term relief for their frustration. The result is those that devote their careers to caring for animals, the shelter employees, are always under attack and continually responding defensively towards the zealots. The situation remains uncorrected. Those with irresponsible animal practices continue to acquire and lose or abandon numerous pets, and they contribute to the cycle where animals rotate into the shelter at alarming, but regular rates. And the ever-constant horror of euthanasia follows along.

What a grim picture. What a difficult place to work day in and day out. Yes, it could be—but it could also be a tremendous opportunity to make a difference. I looked at each shelter staff member as an individual, sought out their interests and expertise. Slowly, I tried to build their trust in me so that they would open up, share their experiences and ideas in order to improve the conditions for the animals, as well as their working environment, and make a better life for everyone. I started with the first group of employees that I had supervisory responsibilities for, the Registered Veterinary Technicians, RVTs.

Jane's Story—Compassion For the Animals

What sort of person does it take to become an RVT in an animal shelter? First of all, they must have a strong passion for animals, use good observation skills, and be able to make decisions and work calmly in emergency situations. As you can tell, they must also have enough self-confidence to take ridicule and harassment from others. This skill set is not always easy to find in an individual. Maybe even more difficult is to find someone with these qualities that can survive for long periods of time in this environment. That's why I was amazed when I met the lead technician at East Valley, Jane.

She was in her 40's, small in stature, and had a short shag haircut. Despite the emergencies she faced daily and her non-stop animal handling, her white uniform shirt was always clean and crisp. One last detail on Jane—she was completely deaf in one ear. Years of kennel work and daily exposure to barking dogs had taken its toll.

The first day I did rounds at that shelter, I noticed her bustling about. She was doing what I later found out was called "taking care of business." That was sort of an understatement when it came to Jane. She could "take care of business" working at the capacity of two to three technicians. I carefully stayed out of her way on that first day and watched the master at work.

The medical room was spotless and highly organized. The cabinets were secured, labeled with their contents, and appropriately stocked. Medical records were completed and filed on each animal. Medical treatment logs were current and accurate. Animals with critical illnesses or injuries were stabilized and housed in the medical room for closer observation and veterinary review.

Jane did not interact with many employees as I watched her. The more I watched, the more I knew why. They just couldn't keep up with her pace, let alone strike up a conversation with her. That is not to say that she didn't work with the kennel staff and the officers. The trucks would roll in from the streets and be full with 6-8 animals ready for entry into the shelter. Some of the animals would not require medical attention, but many did. The officers never had to look for Jane. She knew instinctively what activities were going on within the shelter. The truck would pull up, and Jane would meet the officer on the driver's side. The officer would move to the animal holding compartment in the truck and relay their observations to Jane, and she would assess the animal and usually remove it herself to the medical area for emergency stabilization when needed.

I watched this interaction and could see in the officer's eyes the total confidence they had in her when releasing the animal that they'd just saved off the street into her care. I sat back and said a thank you. How lucky I was to have someone of this caliber working with me.

I waited until Jane took a few seconds' break and approached her with my notebook and questions of animals I had observed in the kennels. She greeted me quickly as she kept walking (never a wasted moment), and we headed for the medical/isolation holding building. I shared my list of observations from the kennels: dogs with snotty noses, those that seemed to be mismatched with their kennel mates and appeared to not be eating, and one dog that was limping. Jane cross-referenced the impound numbers of those animals and her current medical treatment list and found the limping dog on it. The dog was examined upon entry, no fractures were palpated, the injury was documented as soft-tissue, and she was waiting for my arrival today and further assessment for the diagnosis. The dog with the snotty nose just broke with illness that morning, had been in the shelter for over a week with no interest in adoption from the public, and was to be euthanized that day. She said she would move to a new kennel the little dog that was not getting along with the kennel mates and make sure that he ate that morning. We then systematically examined all of the animals in the medical room and reviewed their charts. Jane took care of dispensing all of the medications as directed and kept accurate records for each animal.

In addition to all of this, she'd already re-examined all of the dogs and cats that were adopted the previous day and scheduled for transport that morning to a private veterinary hospital for spay or neuter surgery. The adopters would pick them up at the hospital later in the day (instead of the animals returning to the shelter, awaiting pick up, and taking up valuable kennel space). Spay/neuter outsourcing to private local veterinary hospitals was a great program that ensured all adopted animals would be sterilized. At the same time, outsourcing freed up space in the kennels when animals were transported to the hospital for surgery. Jane noted that all 10 of the dogs and 4 cats remained healthy, vaccinations had been administered, and they were already loaded in the animal control collection vehicle waiting for the ACT to transport.

As I reviewed all of Jane's work for the morning, I found that she'd not missed one detail. Every animal had been seen and cared for and was ready for the day. A day in which another opportunity to be adopted into a permanent home or for their owners to find them would lie ahead. But for others, their future would unfortunately not hold the potential for placement in a loving home.

At a public shelter, the euthanasias are usually completed before the shelter opens up to the public. The East Valley shelter was one of the busiest in the region, and the daily, dreaded task of euthanasia by lethal injection was performed by the RVT and generally completed before 8:00 A.M. But that day I noticed that the process was still ongoing, and it was close to 8:30 A.M.

There are so many details, which have to be considered in the euthanasia process, that are not associated with directly handling the animals. An animal's record is reviewed by at least three supervisory and medical employees to ensure an owner has not been identified, and that there is no adopter or rescue group interested in the animal. The room where the procedure is completed needs to be easily cleaned and contain high-powered hoses and floor drains throughout. It must be safe for the employees with non-slip floors and security for employee entrance and exit. There must be storage space for supplies and equipment, and there must be a sink and an examination table as well as animal holding cages in the room. It is necessary to have a refrigeration area to hold the bodies of the animals after euthanasia. This space must be connected to the euthanasia room with internal and external access. Finally, the external access must have a drive-up ramp to the doorway so that the sanitation truck can pull in and remove the deceased bodies in an acceptable and sanitary manner and transport them to the local rendering facility.

The East Valley shelter was currently undergoing renovation so that they could have an improved euthanasia room. Unfortunately, the construction work was taking close to 4 months and caused the re-location of the euthanasia procedure to a shed that had been placed on the back of the shelter lot as a temporary euthanasia room. In addition, a new and improved refrigeration unit was being installed, which meant that the current storage of deceased bodies was in a unit that was not connected to the euthanasia shed. This detail became crucial when staff had to move euthanized animals from the shed to the refrigeration unit over 500 yards away. Even though this activity was going on in the rear of the shelter, it was still accessible to the public, so it was important that the euthanasias and storage of bodies was completed prior to the shelter being opened to the public.

There were days, however, that were overwhelming in the number of euthanasias, and completion of the task was prolonged after 8:00 A.M. The only way staff could move the bodies from the shed to the refrigeration unit was on carts that were covered with sheets. The fact of the matter was that, at this shelter, it was not uncommon for 70-80 animals to be euthanized daily. This was quite an improvement I was told by staff members who were 15-20 year employees. They remembered a time when 100-120 euthanasias a day were common place. This is something I can't even comprehend.

An annual estimate of euthanasia at this shelter location 20 years ago would be around 33,600 animals. This was only one of six locations in the city. The County of Los Angeles also has six shelters with similar impound numbers which would essentially double these horrific statistics. I am thankful that the veterinary community has stepped up by increasing spay/neuter surgeries and embraced early age spay/neuter (altering animals as early as eight weeks of age so that they are not allowed to have that first litter). This practice has greatly lowered these euthanasia numbers. More on this in later chapters...

What a horrible tragedy, and what a horrible task to ask staff to endure day in and day out—a burden they had to endure for someone else's irresponsibility...

This stressful arrangement of stacking deceased animal bodies on a cart, pushing them to the refrigeration unit, and unloading them, one by one, onto the floor lasted for months. Finally, the renovation was completed, and the staff was able to utilize a new, clean, safe room that had a self-contained refrigeration unit. Many of you may be saying right now that I should be commenting on the animals in this situation, not the employees. I have been a certified euthanasia instructor for many years, and I can tell you that the level of stress for the animal is clearly reflected on the technician(s) in the room. If they are well trained in humane handling techniques and can focus on approaching the animals with empathy rather than be distracted, the animals will also be calmer. The definition of euthanasia is a humane death, and we should be doing everything possible to make sure it truly is humane.

I look back at those months and wonder how the technicians and kennel staff could make it through that difficult time and return to work every day, still caring for each live animal that entered the shelter. I came to know that it was just simply for that very reason. They had made a commitment to look after these animals regardless of whether the animal's stay was 5 days or 60 days. Every animal deserved to be treated the best we could for as long as we could.

People on the outside, non-employees, may complain about shelters, the animals there, and euthanasias, but they have the freedom of coming and going to the shelter dependent on what they can emotionally endure. If it gets too much to bear, they leave, and many do not return for weeks. But if you are an employee, you must return every day. There is no relief. That is the crucial difference. It is easy to be critical when you can escape the stress at will. It is easier if you are only a "weekend warrior."

Euthanasia was one of the greatest stresses in the job, but there were other aspects of my job too, like administrative responsibilities, which included disciplinary action and terminating employees that were high on the stress list. I recall one situation very clearly that materialized soon after my initial appointment to the Chief Veterinarian position. I was called into an executive session with the Commissioners for the Department of Animal Control. I remember this particular occasion because I was called in to discuss the performance of one of my employees. As the situation unfolded in front of me, Jane was being accused of not doing her job properly, but I soon realized the true reason was that they were blaming her for the high euthanasia numbers being reported from the East Valley Shelter.

A newly appointed Commissioner was determined to have her removed from employment, or at least to transfer her to another shelter, and cited what he described as her lack of compassion. A vocal animal rights advocate (with longstanding vendettas against the shelter and any employee who performed euthanasias, which was all of my RVT staff) was directing this particular Commissioner. I knew the commitment and professionalism that Jane brought to the shelter every day and how she relieved the suffering of animals. I knew that if I took the Commissioner on, my life at the shelter would become increasingly more complicated, but I just couldn't allow them to remove Jane. I verbally protested the request, backed up my assessment of Jane with facts and one-on-one observations of her skills. Nevertheless, the Commissioner opposed all that I fought for, but Jane stayed with the department, and she even stayed at the East Valley shelter.

That was my first taste of the bitterness that surrounds shelters. It changed me. I lost a little of my faith in believing that, once people have all of the facts, they will process that information and act in a reasonable manner.

However, there were other benefits to fighting this fight for one of my RVTs. The tale of my actions traveled like wildfire throughout the shelter line staff. We now all had a pact—that I was here to work with them, to guide them and protect them as long as they did their part to make this the best world possible for the animals in our care.

As time passed and Jane understood that I respected her work and would stand up to protect her, she began to let me inside, into her world, but still only in short little snippets. One such example was when I was introduced to a very special non-employee one morning at the East Valley shelter.

Even though some non-employees didn't understand and couldn't relate to the issues surrounding a public shelter, there were still some wonderful people out there that could relate. I recall a woman that I started to see on a regular basis at the shelter. Before I met her, I would catch her looking at me from afar in a worried, untrusting manner. When our eyes would meet, she would quickly look away and lower her head so that her hair would fall in front of her face and obscure her view. I often saw her talking quietly to Jane, off in a far corner of the shelter. The woman seemed to be quite serious about their whispers, yet comfortable with Jane.

One day, I was in the euthanasia room with Jane and the soft spoken woman confidently entered the room. She was shocked to see me there and froze with a large, unruly purebred dog at the end of a lead. Jane quickly moved forward and said to the woman, "It's alright. She's O.K. You don't have to worry." At that moment, I realized I had earned Jane's trust, and I had been pulled into the employee circle. I nodded at the woman and didn't interfere, but just observed how she and Jane interacted together.

I shook my head in agreement and watched the two women handle an extremely aggressive dog that was three-quarters their weight. As a team, they performed a restraint move on the dog by partially opening a door, weaving the lead through the door jam as they sandwiched the dog between the door and the wall. Before the dog knew what happened, Jane pumped a tranquilizer into his rear leg muscle. Jane expertly grabbed the leash, in full control of this animal, and tricked him into walking into a large holding cage. Then we all waited for the tranquilizer to take effect.

The woman quickly explained that this was another one (another of the breed that she was committed to rescuing) that she had been contacted about by the owner. I took a look at the 90-plus pound dog, who continued to address all of us in the room with a deep, continuous growl. The woman continued, "I just don't understand what these people think is going to happen. He is only two years of age, not neutered, and they have been keeping him in the backyard for months without touching him because they are afraid of him. I had to go in the backyard and get him with a pole, they were so scared of him. God, these people are idiots! The poor thing! I am full at my house with good natured rescue dogs. What am I gonna do with him if I can't adopt him out?" I later found out that this wonderful rescue person had at least 10-15 dogs rotating through her personal kennels that she was adopting out to responsible owners. She had such a tremendous commitment and respect for this breed she loved.

Jane looked at her reassuringly. "I know. We wouldn't adopt him out of the shelter either." She turned to me and said, "Owners call her hoping that she will take these purebreds that they have spent over a thousand dollars on and can no longer handle. They want someone else to take on the responsibility, the liability, of finding them homes, or find the strength to euthanize them."

The woman became more talkative as she continued to justify the action they were preparing to start. "I talk to them over the phone and usually tell them that the best thing to do for the dog is to put them to sleep. They are usually relieved to hear it from someone else. They sign ownership of the animal to me, and I bring them into the shelter, and as the owner, I request they be euthanized. Lot of people don't understand that this breed is abused out there, adopted for the wrong reasons, especially if a gang banger finds out the dog is real mean. I love these dogs too much to let them go through that kind of abuse. Yes, this is much better, much more humane for them."

In about ten minutes, the dog in the cage was laying flat out, with his enormous head resting on his front paws and plastered against the cage door with this tongue hanging out of the side of his mouth. Jane moved in cautiously, with euthanasia solution in hand. She gently muzzled the big boy and quickly placed a tourniquet on his front leg, causing the cephalic vein to stand out, coursing over the limb. She expertly placed the needle in the vein and drew back on the syringe, which filled with blood indicating that she had a clean "stick." She released the tourniquet and injected the deep blue solution. The dog released one last combination growl-groan, and his head dropped one final time. We waited. Within a few seconds, Jane checked the eyes which had no palpebral response. She reached for his inner rear leg to check a pulse and found none. The woman moved toward Jane and the dog and said, "Sorry big guy, but this was the best thing for ya."

The two women no longer spoke. One took the front legs, the other, the rear legs, and they clumsily carried the dog to the refrigeration area about ten feet away and placed him on the floor. They closed the door, Jane completed the paperwork on the animal, they nodded at each other, the woman nodded at me, and she quietly left the room.

Jane looked up from her writing and said to me, "That is one special lady to care that much for that breed. The animals she picks up from these owners, no one else would take. Those dogs would probably sit in those backyards for years with no human contact if it weren't for her. Or maybe, they would end up selling them to people looking for guard dogs or dogs they could use as sparing dogs for pit bull fights. She is quite a lady. Too bad so many people don't understand that what she does actually protects the breed."

In Jane's own abrupt way, she quickly left me alone in the room—alone to step back and assess what had just happened. Was that what people meant by secrets at the shelter? Perhaps so. This was one secret that, even when explained, is difficult for people to understand. This action, however, serves to protect the animals that man has bred and brought into this world without a care for the animal's final resting place. Unfortunately, Jane was probably correct. Many would not understand how humane this action truly was.

Norman's Story—a Long-term Resident

It is true that the majority of time devoted to animal care involves dogs and cats. However, in addition to the traditional dogs and cats that everyone thinks of being housed in an animal shelter, there actually is a variety of other animals that are cared for in these facilities. As a matter of fact, you can find reptiles, birds, rodents, and large animals like horses, and even pot bellied pigs and goats. Whenever I think of goats, I always think of the mascot at the East Valley shelter, Norman. I say this with a grain of salt—Norman, what a treasure...

Norman the Goat was white in color, overweight, spoiled rotten, and in need of dehorning. I don't really know how Norman came to reside permanently at the shelter, but my guess is that he was brought into the facility on a humane case, the owner either decided not to claim him or was not allowed to take him, and there were no interested adopters. Many animals involved with humane seizures end up staying at shelters for long periods of time (sometimes up to a year) waiting for the legal formalities to be completed or run their course. During the holding period, many staff members get attached to these animals, and many either adopt them, or in rare cases, the animal(s) end up living at the animal shelter. Norman happened to be just such a case. He was unique and created a great deal of conversation between members of the public and staff when they observed him in his corral.

Many of the staff enjoyed feeding and caring for Norman, and he liked them too. The Senior Animal Care Technician (ACT) even had a professionally framed photograph of Norman on his desk. My understanding is that Norman was taken down to the local pet store one Christmas season when they were photographing people's pets for holiday cards. Norman posed handsomely with the picturesque backdrop behind him, much like in the photos you see of children that were taken in department stores and end up being displayed in the wallets of proud parents.

You see, I never could really understand this infatuation for ol' Norman. Norman never really liked me very much, and every chance he could get, he chased me, tried to butt me, and just got that anxious look in his eyes and always made me the object of his frustrations whenever I was around him. You may ask, "Why would you keep such an animal at the shelter?" Good question, and one I asked staff every time I had an interaction with Norman.

One Monday in particular comes to mind when I was making the rounds at the East Valley shelter, and the facility was closed to the public. With no public on the grounds, Norman was allowed to roam freely on the compound to get some much-needed exercise. I entered the shelter from the administration building that day and walked straight through and to the outdoor animal holding areas. I was looking for the RVT on duty and at the same time was observing dogs as I walked by the kennels when I stopped in my tracks. I was looking down at the ground on the walkway between the kennels, and to my horror, I saw it—I saw goat droppings. That could only mean one thing. Norman was somewhere near, and he was loose and unsupervised. My face got a little flushed, and despite putting on my athlete endurance antiperspirant that morning, I could feel moisture accumulating under my arms. I took a quick visual of the enclosed kennel area I was standing in, and it appeared safe—no Norman.

I moved a few paces forward and approached the end of the holding area and there, right there, peering around the corner with an evil glare, was NORMAN! We both froze and stared at each other for about 5 seconds that seemed like 10 minutes. Then Norman made the first move. He never did anything slowly or with question. He bolted out from around the corner and bee-lined directly for me. I was quite thankful that I'd earned a collegiate letter in track, and I spun around and took off, running down the outside section of the kennels. Norman was in hot pursuit, with his head down and his horns clearly in view. Norman may have had good instincts, but I was smarter than him (or at least at that moment I told myself I had to be). I ducked into a doorway and watched Norman cruise right by, unable to stop himself in time to make the sharp right turn.

I didn't wait, however. I motored through the remainder of the indoor kennel, broke my way free to the outside, and put it in high gear for the administration building. I saw the door, reached for it, made my way inside, and caught my breath. I looked out the window, and there was Norman, a bit slower than me, but he had been hot on my heels and was standing in front of the door. He didn't seem disappointed. He slowly walked around the area where he last had me in his sights, grazed a bit on the only small patch of grass on the compound, and then moseyed back to the kennel area. He knew there would be another day, another chase, and another opportunity to show the Doc who was boss at the East Valley shelter!

"Norman" the goat poses for a portrait at Christmas. This portrait could be found on the desk of the Animal Care Technician Supervisor for the East Valley Shelter.

Chapter Two:
South Los Angeles Shelter, L.A., California

Realities and Traditions...

The very first day I arrived in Los Angeles, I was escorted from shelter to shelter by one of the administrative analysts who had previously worked in the field at all six locations. She tried to put a positive spin on what we were about to see, but as we exited off the I-10 freeway into the heart of South Los Angeles, I became increasingly more anxious about what I was about to encounter. We drove down the busy street of Crenshaw, passing by home style barbecue restaurants, heavily gated car repair shops, and several houses of worship with male church members on the sidewalks in fluorescent suits spreading the word of the Lord. The smell of local eateries filled the air, and all places of business were busy with people everywhere.

We approached a side street and turned off the main drag of Crenshaw. We now were in a residential neighborhood with small, single, well-kept dwellings. A bright purple house caught my eye on the left side of the street, for it stood out on the entire block. Soon after that, we made a right, and the dilapidated shelter was on the left side of the street. Across the street was a dairy distribution center with large semi trucks parked out front. This block was entirely industrial. There was no color anywhere to be seen. I had the urge to run down the block and take one last look at the purple house, so I could remember what color looked like, but instead, I remained motionless in the front seat of the car.

We turned into the gated parking area and found a parking place. We were surrounded by cement. Old, damaged lockers were placed in the lot (apparently awaiting pick up and disposal). Every surface was covered with dirt and debris, and the entrance to the gate had a hand-written sign carelessly taped to it showing the hours of operation.

Before we got out of the car, my tour guide continued to lecture me on the history of the South Central animal shelter. Whenever she wanted to really make a point, she would bellow out the words, placing strong emphasis on them by raising the decibel at which she was speaking by about three notches. "This building is so old and outdated that the Los Angeles SPCA (Society for the Prevention of Cruelty to Animals) got out of it in the 1930's and SOLD IT TO ANIMAL CONTROL. Then, about two years ago, the building sustained so much damage from the L.A. earthquake that portions were CONDEMNED."

She pointed to a forward section of the building that was roped off and had signs pasted to the doorways, "Do Not Enter, use entrance ahead." She went on to explain that the administration building was closed down after the quake and that all of the offices and the clerical area had been moved to the former spay/neuter clinic, which was the building farthest from the lot we were parked in. What she didn't tell me was that probably the entire complex should have been bulldozed, because the animal holding area and clinic area didn't appear to be fit for man or beast.

She said that plans to construct a new South Los Angeles shelter were in the works, but she added that they had been working on this for about two to three years. The project was complicated because, first, the city needed to identify an additional site to build a temporary shelter. Then the city had to complete plans to build that temporary shelter (probably taking a year or so), relocate all of the animals from the current shelter, take down the current buildings, and then build the new state-of-the-art building. She said, "In other words, don't count on any CHANGES TOO SOON."

We got out of the car and walked towards the animal holding area of the shelter. As I passed through the cement gate, I noticed that numerous cracks could be found on the walls, driveway, and doorways. I found myself standing in a 10-foot by 12-foot breezeway (if you could call it that) made of cement. To my left were about 70 dog kennels of various size. To my right were doorways to two different buildings, one of which was the cattery. Straight ahead of me was a doorway with the faded words, Medical Room, painted on the frame. The door was closed, but you could hear a great deal of activity on the other side. The shelter was open to the public after 8:00 A.M. Since it was early, we made our way to the building easily. My tour guide and I approached the medical room, opened the door, and walked in. I was not prepared for what I was about to see.

I scanned the small examination room. It had cabinets and counter space on one side and an old-fashioned, glass-faced, floor-to-ceiling medical cabinet on the other side. There was a stainless steel examination table in the middle of the room that took up most of the space, with the result that only one person at at time could pass on either side of the table. The room was covered with blood all over the floor—drops of blood, drag marks of blood... The counter tops were dirty and blood-spotted, with vials of medications, a bottle of euthanasia solution, and numerous syringes and needles scattered about.

There were two other people in the room with us, and we could barely all fit and move about the area. One was an Animal Care Attendant (ACT) who had brought in a pit bull-cross. Instead of using leashes like most pet owners are used to, staff were issued rope leads. They provided the strength and stiffness needed to control all sizes of animals. The rope lead also did double duty after it was placed around the neck of the animal. The remaining long end of the rope could be used as a customized muzzle when humanely secured around the snout of a dog.

The ACT had a rope muzzle on the dog, restraining him on the floor for euthanasia. The Registered Veterinary Technician (RVT), with syringe and needle in hand, performed the euthanasia, and the dog quickly slid to the ground. The RVT checked the heart rate and pronounced the dog dead, and the ACT dragged the dog to the next room, which was the refrigeration area for the dead bodies. I followed the trail of blood from the still oozing venipuncture and saw a pile of dogs and cats at least 40 in number. I stood for a moment in shock. The odors of fresh blood, feces, and wet animal hair coats surrounded me.

I left this room knowing that I needed to see everything before I made any comments and proceeded into a medical holding area adjacent to the medical room. There were no windows in this room, which was actually a hallway. The rolling cages were old and had obviously been pieced together, and ill and injured animals with wrapped limbs were looking out of the cage doors with hopeful eyes.

I moved through this hallway into the main dog holding area. The kennels were prehistoric, but at least they had indoor and outdoor sections with a very small, narrow opening cut in the cement that the dogs could move through. The opening could be closed off with a guillotine door. This door helped separate animals from the two sections if a fight arose, or divided the space for daily cleaning to try to keep animals dry. This area exemplified what it must have been like to live in a dungeon—dark, musty, and everywhere you looked there were hard surfaces. The animal feeders were in place in all of the kennels, and small wild birds were constantly trying to sneak kibble and taunting the dogs. As a result, there were bird droppings on the kennel floors and bars, as well as throughout the walkways.

After I recorded in my brain the physical restrictions of this facility, I started to focus on the animals. I moved through the dogs and could barely recognize one dog from the next. Were they all Shepherd and pit bull crosses, weighing about 60-70 pounds, filthy and thin? Upon closer examination, I noted that on the female side, most had mammary glands that were stretched and hanging to the floor. How many litters had these poor animals endured? Their own bodies were thin, even emaciated, which painted the picture for me of their unpleasant past and uncertain future. Who would adopt these animals? And there were over a hundred within my view, crammed into

50-60 kennels. No wonder they had to euthanize so many daily. They couldn't possibly maintain 5-6 per kennel in these conditions. They would either starve, because the dominant dogs wouldn't allow the submissive ones to eat, or they would be attacked and killed once pack behavior set in and the weakest was chosen. I took a deep breath and closed my eyes for a second, hoping when I opened them that it would all be different—but it wasn't.

I left the kennel area and moved across the breezeway towards the other buildings. I moved to the area where the dangerous dogs (dogs with a history of biting or attacking) were housed away from the public. The door was open, but a chain was placed across the doorway forbidding admittance to the public. The room had six kennels in it that were all indoors. The room was dark and damp, making it all the more eerie. I approached some of the dogs, who immediately charged the kennel gate due to my presence, slobbered, and viciously attacked the bars, hoping to have just a few seconds of freedom to take me down. I was startled and jumped back from the kennel gate and then regained my focus.

I approached the kennel gates again and observed some of the largest pit bulls I had ever seen in my life. These dogs were 90-100 pounds easily—huge intact males with enough testosterone to take on the world. I became horrified at the thought that a dog like this might be roaming the streets loose and unattended. Such a dog could easily kill a child, severely injure an adult, and definitely kill another dog or cat. Could these animals ever be integrated back into society? My next thought was, how does the kennel staff handle these animals, clean them, and feed them? I couldn't imagine the stress on the employees who were assigned to caring for these animals.

The Best Cats Anywhere

I moved to the next building, which had an open door, and to my relief it was the cattery. The room's perimeter was lined with cages, all of different sizes and manufacturers. This room, too, had been pieced together. In the center of the room were some rabbits that were comfortably housed. As I moved from cage to cage, I was elated to see that these were some of the most beautiful and healthy cats I had ever seen—gorgeous Siamese cats, domestic short-haired cats with the bluest eyes that seem to pierce right through you... As I approached them, each began to purr loudly, just wanting to be petted and stroked. They rose from their lounging positions and rubbed up against the bars of the cage doors awaiting a human touch. Several reached out from in between the cage bars, trying to get my attention, and batted me as I walked by. What wonderful personalities these animals had and what wonderful pets they would make for some fortunate family.

Of course there were many adults, but there were also cages full of nursing queens with 5-6 kittens each, and all appeared healthy and thriving. I looked up to the ceiling of the building and noticed that many of the ceiling tiles were missing and the attic area above was exposed. I quietly wondered to myself why this building had not also been condemned and how much asbestos could be found in that ceiling. Then it dawned on me why everyone in this room was so healthy. The door to the room remained open much of the time, and the fresh air helped maintain a healthy environment. I also knew that, if these cats had survived on the streets of South Los Angeles with the disease exposures there, then they certainly had built up immunities, and they seemed to remain healthy in the shelter cattery. At other shelters, where the cats were confined to closed rooms without fresh air, they became sick, and soon the entire room was exposed to disease, which resulted in lower adoptions and increased euthanasias.

As a result of this very first tour of the South Los Angeles shelter cattery, I always directed potential adopters from anywhere in the city to the South Central shelter to adopt cats. My first impression remained sound that they were the healthiest and most beautiful cats of all of our shelters. As a matter of fact, when my in-laws were looking for a cat to adopt after their 20-year-old cat had to be euthanized, I went to the South Central shelter with my husband and picked out a gorgeous flame point Siamese with radiant blue eyes. This guy grew into a huge, lovable companion for them and created hours of entertainment for the grandchildren.

Do-it-yourself Animal Care

After walking through the cat area, my hopes were semi-restored, and I ventured back into the medical room. The employees appeared to have completed the scheduled euthanasias for that morning. All of the animals had been removed from the room, and the floors were in the process of being mopped. I walked into the adjacent room that housed the walk-in cooler for body storage. The stack of bodies had been re-located from the floor to the cooler. I introduced myself to the RVT on duty, and it was obvious that my tour guide had talked to him when I ventured away from the medical room briefly. He was an older man, and I later learned that he had been with the department for over 20 years. He didn't go through the schooling and testing for his California veterinary technician license, but was grandfathered in and received certification due to his years of hands-on experience. I also understood that he was scheduled to retire within the coming month.

He checked me out in an untrusting manner and said, "You know, we just has to kill these animals on account that their owners don't take care of them. We just don't got the room to keep them all here—too many of them coming in all day and all night long—especially at kitten and puppy season."

I responded that I knew there was a tremendous problem with irresponsible owners, but I also wanted to review the protocols of how animals were handled prior to euthanasia. I made it very clear to him that, from this day forward, we would never drag animals to the euthanasia area. We would either pick up non-leash-trained animals or use gurneys or carts to transport them.

He looked at me and said, "You don't understand. Here in South L.A., we do 80-90 animals a day. That's gonna take lots of extra time."

I told him that, once we got used to the new protocol, it would be easier on everyone, and it would also help us ensure respect for the animals and our jobs. He hung his head low and did not interact with me any further.

That was the first and last time I interacted with that particular employee. He was the last of a generation that was being replaced at the shelter by younger, more open-minded, and compassionate RVTs. Within months, I hired an Animal Control Officer (ACO) who was a veterinarian from the Phillipines. He was licensed in California to practice in the capacity of an RVT. He had earned a great deal of respect at the South Central shelter as an ACO, and as he transitioned to the veterinary medical division, he became one of the top contributors, rekindling dignity and empathy at the shelter. Marty was reliable and used his law enforcement assessment skills in decision making on a daily basis. He made the shelter a better environment for the animals and the staff. He also was a regular participant in our community vaccine clinics. One of the top reasons I so admired Marty was that, several times, I offered to transfer him to a different shelter that didn't perform as many euthanasias, but he always refused the transfer. He said he knew he was needed at South Central, and this was home for him.

Before I left the medical room that day, I encountered an animal control officer with a black lab-cross puppy in his arms, standing in the doorway. He greeted the RVT warmly and then looked at me in a questioning manner. As soon as I introduced myself to him, he seemed relieved and placed the puppy on the exam table in the middle of the room.

I touched this very depressed and weak puppy, and when I looked at the palm of my hand, it was covered with a sticky, thick, black material. The RVT said, "He's covered in motor oil." I looked at him in astonishment, and he continued, "They all do that around here. They think it gets rid of the mange."

I responded, "Well, they are right about one thing. It certainly kills every mite on their skin, but it also acts as a toxin on the animal." That's why that little guy was so depressed and listless. We bathed the puppy, trying to remove as much of the motor oil as possible. We also tried administering fluids to him, but eventually, the puppy was humanely euthanized. I had never heard of anyone doing this to a dog in order to control mange. I knew I had so much to learn.

Before we could even finish caring for the puppy, another pair of officers came rolling into the breezeway with their patrol vehicle filled with animals. They called me out to look at one of the dogs in the middle compartment. The officer had a smile on his face, so I knew this was going to be another test of my "street" knowledge. He opened the outer door of one of the animal holding compartments, and as I peered through the bars of the cage door, I saw a fairly large brown pit bull with jagged cropped ears that were flush to her skull. Her tail was beating against the back of the cage, and I knew from her body language that she was quite friendly.

As he opened the cage door, I couldn't help but notice that she had a five-pound weight hanging from the collar around her neck. I was stunned and could only imagine the strength it would take to drag around that extra weight on her neck all day and all night long. The officer asked me why I thought the weight was around her neck. I was sure that some kids had taken advantage of her and placed the weight around her neck as a sort of sick joke and act of animal cruelty. The officer's response painted a reality that few of us would have thought of. He said he was called out to a property where the neighbors had complained about the treatment of the dogs. When he arrived, he found this young, female pit bull with the five-pound plate around her neck. The neighbors said that the female constantly jumped over the fence from the owner's yard and got into their yard and roamed in the street. The owners couldn't afford to build a higher fence, so they placed the five-pound weight around her neck so that she couldn't make it over the fence. They solved the problem, saved money, and still maintained their dog in the yard to protect the property.

I was stunned. It was amazing how the people in this community would problem-solve—first the motor oil on dogs with mange, now strapping weights on dogs to stop them from jumping over fences. The officer reached over to this gentle, obedient dog and pulled the weight from her neck. I watched her as the weight was lifted. The muscles in her neck relaxed, her head rose to its normal carriage, and she tested her new-found freedom by moving her head with ease from side to side and then up and down again. The officer was standing at waist-high level with her because she was still in the vehicle's holding compartment, and she reached over and promptly licked his hand, tail still wagging, and now her entire body was wiggling in rhythm with her tail motion.

It was so different from being in private veterinary practice. People on the streets took animal care into their own hands. Sometimes that meant concocting their own treatment regimens or trying to be resourceful in maintaining their pet, and other times it meant abandoning their pet in hopes that someone else would take on the responsibility and the monetary expense of caring for the animal. There was something exhilarating about this new facet of education. It was real, it wasn't a textbook, it was hands-on, and I liked the challenge. How lucky I was to have six shelters of teachers who learned from experience and could show me the ropes.

My tour guide motioned to me and pointed at her wristwatch, indicating that our time at South Central was over for today and that we needed to move on. After only a few hours there, I no longer was uncomfortable, and I actually wanted to stay. I felt something that I never experienced in small animal private practice—the tremendous need for veterinary support for animals that everyone else had conveniently forgotten—the abandoned, unwanted, and abused. Certainly, it was much easier to care for owned animals where bills were paid and recovered animals were returned to their permanent homes. But this was so different, almost abstract and intangible. This was an opportunity to make a difference, and to get what gratification one could receive by truly helping those who needed it the most.

The Heartbreak of the Day-to-day

What an introduction to a diverse and animal-overpopulated area! My first visit was not extraordinary, but actually fairly normal at the South L.A. shelter. After several months on the job, I remember being pulled out of an administrative meeting at 9:00 A.M. because one of the ACTs from the South L.A. shelter needed to speak with me on the phone. I left the meeting and took the call in my administrative office located in downtown L.A. on the thirteenth floor of an old city-owned high rise building. The ACT spoke quickly and frantically. "Doc, you gotta come right away. The RVT din't show up today, and luckily it's Monday and we're closed to the public. But we got 80 or so animals to euthanize. If we wait until tomorrow to do it, we will have double that to do, and there ain't no way we can do all of that in one day. You gotta hurry up and get here."

"O.K.," I said, "I understand. I will be there in less than an hour."

"Just hurry" was the reply.

The South L.A. shelter was a 25-minute drive from downtown on a good traffic day, down one of the busiest freeways in the country, the Santa Monica freeway. When I arrived and pulled into an empty parking space, I was greeted by the ACT who phoned me, and he barely let me get out of my city-issued vehicle. "We've been waiting for you. Where you been?" he asked anxiously. "I got dogs lined up. We gotta get started."

I quickly followed him to the medical room, and he wasn't kidding. He had ACTs lined up holding dogs on leads waiting to be euthanized. It was at that moment that I knew I didn't truly know what I was getting myself into when I told my RVT staff that I would need to experience their job in order to make decisions about new programs of animal care. I assumed I would have to perform some euthanasia, but I don't think anyone could have been prepared for what was in store for me that morning at the South Los Angeles shelter.

I told the ACTs that I needed a minute to get into the controlled substance lock box where the euthanasia solution was securely stored, get together other equipment like syringes and needles, and set up the daily euthanasia log. I was ready within 3-4 minutes and the first dog was led through the hallway of the medical holding area into the tiny medical room. The dog looked like every dog I had seen in the kennel previously. He was about 50 pounds, tan and black with erect ears, an intact male, underweight, dirty with a mild hair loss over the tail head and his chest, indicative of a flea allergy dermatitis and or mange, wearing a worn-out dark-colored collar with no identification on it. I asked the ACT to put the dog on the stainless steel table for examination.

He took a deep breath and said, "Doc, maybe you don't understand, I got about 80 dogs for you to do. We can't be lifting each one of them on this table for you, or we ain't never gonna get done today. It don't matter if they have a sickness or not. They have been here past the holding period, their owners ain't coming for them, nobody wants to adopt them, and they have been signed off for euthanasia by the Lieutenant. Anyway, we brought in 60 new dogs yesterday and only adopted out six, and my kennels are full with 3-5 dogs per kennel. So far this morning, I have impounded ten puppies without their mama, and nine adult dogs from the public. That don't even count what the ACOs will bring from the streets this morning. The trucks ain't been back to the shelter yet."

I was silent. This was all so wrong, but it was too obvious that there were no options. Were we going to keep these dogs? What about the dogs that had been here less time and were sitting in their kennel. Did they deserve to die today instead? Something had to give, we were out of space, and no one wanted to take these dogs.

I knelt down to the dog and quickly examined him by running my fingers over his body and following the path with my eyes. The ACT handed me the dog's impound card and called out the number on the tag the dog was wearing attached to the chain collar around his neck. I confirmed that the number was the same on the card and the written description matched the dog in front of me. I checked the impound date and counted days to the current day to double check that the legal holding period had been allotted this animal and the appropriate approval signature was on the card. I then turned to the counter and awkwardly grabbed the syringe and needle. I inserted it into the top of the euthanasia solution bottle and pulled up enough milliliters of the "blue juice" to humanely euthanize a dog of this size.

I turned around and faced the dog on the floor. The handler already had the dog comfortably muzzled with the rope lead and was restraining him and presenting the front limb to me for injection. The dog was calm and I gently grabbed the limb with my left hand to steady it as I located the cephalic vein with the index finger of my right hand. Once the vein was isolated, I slipped the large gauge needle into the vein, drew back on the syringe and watched the backflow of blood, indicating I was clearly in the vein, then injected the solution with one smooth, consistent push. After removing the needle, I continued to steady the limb and hold off the puncture site to prevent external blood loss. As I watched, within five seconds of the injection, the body of the dog became limp and his head fell to one side and was cradled by the biceps muscle of the ACT. I instinctively reached for the rear limb to check for a pulse and could not find one. I took my index finger and touched the right eyelid that was now half closed, and this stimulus did not produce a blink response from the dog. The ACT looked at me and said, "Just watch the tail. You will know if he's gone."

"What do you mean?" I asked him.

"I will show you on the next one."

Indeed, that morning, he had many opportunities to show me what he meant. As each dog was euthanized, you could see the tail raise and then slowly lower below the normal carriage position, until it was limp and hung below the body of the dog—yet another indicator of death.

After each dog was euthanized, the body had to be moved about ten feet to the refrigeration area. It was too time consuming to place each dog into the refrigerator immediately after euthanasia, so they were piled in the adjoining room, out of view of each animal that was to be euthanized.

Upon moving the dead animals, often times there would be bleeding from the injection site, urination, and defecation. We never dragged any animals to the euthanasia room. If they were non-ambulatory, they were carried if possible or placed on a gurney. However, once an animal was pronounced dead, it became impossible, impractical (due to the high number of animals euthanized daily), and a risk for employees (on-the-job back injury from lifting) to not drag bodies away from the euthanasia room. I would look up between euthanasias, as I loaded my next syringe, to see drag marks on the floor of blood and feces prior to a quick cleaning in-between animals.

Washing your hands between animals was unheard of. Wearing plastic gloves generally slowed you down and made you clumsy when loading the syringe and writing on the animal's impound card. However, animals with known cases of zoonotic diseases (diseases transmitted from animals to man) like ringworm did necessitate the use of plastic gloves. Each impound or cage card had to indicate the date, time, and number of milliliters of euthanasia solution administered to the animal, along with the initials of either the RVT or veterinarian that performed the euthanasia. These records were mandatory by law, and we strictly adhered to them.

Some of the dogs were small, and they were placed on the stainless steel table for euthanasia. I talked to each one of the animals, trying to keep them calm and give some truth to the meaning of the word "euthanasia," or humane death, in even this horrific environment. The ACT staff accepted my way and knew I needed that extra few seconds of comforting in order to complete the grueling task at hand.

Yes, we euthanized many, many dogs—but cats had even lower adoption rates and were also euthanized in high numbers. Unfortunately, it is very difficult to give intravenous injections to cats due to the very small size of the vein for one, but also due to the temperament of cats. Add to that the smell of dogs that permeated the euthanasia room, and the cats could hear the relentless barking of hundreds of dogs in the nearby kennel. How I wished I could have eliminated this stress for these cats, but there was no other secure, non-public space in which to perform this procedure. This is often the case in most publicly operated shelters—lack of space and dilapidated buildings. All any of us could do was to comfort the cats as much as possible and perform euthanasia by intraperitoneal injection (IP).

Most cats had euthanasia solution injected into their peritoneal space, which surrounds the abdominal area and is then slowly absorbed through the animal's system causing death. Cats were injected and placed in cages for observation and confirmation of death, usually within about 10 minutes of injection. The cats would generally move to the back of the cage and lie down and slowly fall asleep. I personally hated to watch this, and whenever I could, I would try for a vein on a cat. But often times, the cat just wouldn't allow the restraint, and IP injection ended up being less stressful. Cats scheduled for euthanasia were always done separately from the dogs in hopes of easing the stress on them.

On that particular day, I had only finished with the dog euthanasias, and several hours had gone by since my arrival. I told the kennel staff I needed a break and some fresh air as I looked at the stack of impound cards I had in my hand, a stack which indicated the number of dogs we had just euthanized. I looked at the euthanasia log sheet and began counting down the left column, one, two... forty-two, forty-three... sixty-four, sixty-five... and then finally my count ended at eighty-two dogs. Even with that count, it didn't really register on me until, on my way out the door to take a break before coming back to face the cat list, I looked into the refrigeration holding room. To my horror, dead dog carcasses were piled on the cement floor as high as my thighs. Their heads were facing in all directions. I couldn't identify one dog's legs from another's. Eighty-two dogs lay in front of me, and I had killed them all.

I gasped for air, my eyes filled with tears, and I ran from the room into the breezeway to the sounds and smells of hundreds of animals on either side of me that would soon face similar fates. I felt trapped, I began to hyperventilate, and I had to close my eyes to regain a normal breathing cycle. I became filled with anger. How could these God awful people make us do this every day? Those disgusting, irresponsible people who don't care enough for their pets to come looking for them or to spay and neuter them! As my brain continued to move forward now at warp speed, it became all too clear that this was just an ordinary day at the South L.A. shelter. This day of death occurred every single day, every week, every month. How could my RVTs endure this continually? The level of post traumatic stress was incomprehensible.

Facing the On-going War

Over the next few months, I was able to figure out how shelter employees coped with performing this high number of euthanasias. By standing side by side with these employees, holding animals through the euthanasia, and performing euthanasias myself with them, I came to understand the unspoken bond that was established. A unity is established between all that work in that room together, one that allows you to survive it all somehow. If that unity is ever broken, the stress becomes insurmountable, and the result can be deadly for the employee. There are stories of suicide among shelter employees for this very reason—the breakdown of the support system. Their ability to access euthanasia solution and deliver the deadly fluid into their own bodies becomes the only way out for some. Fortunately, that is a rare event. Usually staff members are supportive of one another.

It was my job to monitor staff—to make sure they remained emotionally balanced when performing euthanasias and after they were completed. I looked around the euthanasia rooms at various shelters and saw that staff tried to release their stress by cutting out pictures of friendly puppies and kittens and affixing them to cabinets and walls of the room. Many of the shelters had either hand-painted messages or excerpts from books and magazines that we cut out and taped above the doorway of the refrigeration units: "Rest in Peace my friend..."

or "Your next stop is Heaven." There has never been and there will never be a question in my mind, how very much these people care for each one of the animals that passed through the doorway and into their arms one final time. For some of these animals, it was the only moment of their short and abused lives that they ever received love and compassion.

Thank you to each and every shelter employee that finds it in their hearts to perform this task with kindness and dignity. Your gracious ways do not go unnoticed in the eyes of people who understand why it is being done. But most importantly, you have spent time on this Earth providing kindness and humane care for the unwanted and abandoned animals of your community, and for that, you will reap untold rewards. Stand proud and know that every animal that you have touched has been a blessing, and an act above and beyond the call of duty, for anyone who calls him or herself a human being.

Even though I will never forget the sights, sounds, and smells of that awful day at South Central L.A., it was my most valuable training day—a day to feel compassion for the animals and the staff, to treat the animals kindly up to their last breath of life, to relieve their suffering, to prevent any further abuse they may have endured on the streets, and to be even more determined to fight to help these creatures. There was no doubt in my mind that we were all engaged in a terrible war—a war against irresponsible pet owners who care very little for life—often times animal and/or human. With war, there will be casualties. But as I moved through the following days and months, I hoped we could keep those casualties to a minimum—but as of yet, it still isn't so.

The South L.A. shelter has a special place in my heart. If you have a shelter in your community that sounds similar to South L.A., don't turn your back on it just because it is old, falling apart, and not esthetically pleasing. The animals there do not judge on appearances, and the clock is ticking for them. All you need to do is adopt your next pet from there, and you have suddenly become part of the solution. If everyone did just that, I believe we could call a truce in this bloody war.

Chapter Three:
West Valley Shelter, Chatsworth, California

The Perfect Mouser

The West Valley shelter was located in Chatsworth, at the North tip of the Los Angeles city limits. The drive out to the West Valley was a long one, just about from anywhere, due to the congested freeways. In the Summer, it was always over 95 degrees during the day, and in the Winter, the staff wore turtle necks or long underwear under their city uniforms. You did get the feel you were out in the country, with evidence of horse property, riding stables, and homes with greater spreads of land attached to them. Of all six shelters, this location had a comfortable openness to it. A large portion of the shelter property in the back was devoted to grassy pastures and some stalls for large animals. The employee parking lot smelled of hay and alfalfa, and everything seemed cleaner and crisper.

The shelter itself was in better condition then the South L.A. or East Valley shelters. The administration building housing the clerks and animal control officers was detached from the actual kennel and cattery holding areas. As with all animal holding areas, the dogs were separated by gender on either side of the building. This was done so that more than one dog could be housed in the same kennel at once. If you mixed males and females, there would be unwanted breeding going on 24 hours a day since over 90% of dogs entering a public shelter are intact and usually looking for a mate.

This shelter was the second largest (second to the most modern shelter in the city, North Central) in regards to holding capacity for small animals (dogs and cats), and it had the largest holding capacity for large animals. It also had the second highest adoption rate for all of the city animal shelters.

Not only did the shelters differ in size, their location seemed to attract a different personality of employee. Oversight and management of each shelter was the responsibility of the law enforcement division of animal control. These shelter supervisor positions were limited (one per shelter), and once a high-ranking officer (Lieutenant) filled the position, he or she usually remained there until retirement.

One of the most knowledgeable and helpful Lieutenants that I worked with seemed to be juggled from East to West Valley. He was the most comfortable at West Valley, and that's where I spent most of my time learning from him. Lieutenant Folsom was a very handsome, physically fit man in his fifties. He treated everyone with the respect that they earned and gave everyone under his command every opportunity to succeed and become the best at their job. He nurtured young animal control officers (ACOs) when they needed it and instituted disciplinary action on them when they deserved it.

But what was so clear when you met Lieutenant Folsom was that he loved his job. He loved law enforcement, he respected people and animals, and he was willing to share his experience of 30+ years with all that were receptive. I must say that I never missed an opportunity to visit with the Lieutenant whenever I came out to West Valley, or to call him on the phone if ever I had a legal or policy question. I was confident that he would always steer me in the right direction and that I could trust him. I have a great deal of respect for him and owe him so much for the time and investment he made in me to become the best shelter veterinarian that I could be.

Once your family and friends learn that you work at an animal shelter, you are frequently asked to find them "the perfect pet." Now that's a lot of pressure considering this decision can have an impact lasting over a decade, and I certainly couldn't assure anyone a timeline on when I would find the animal they requested. Since I was constantly moving through six shelters, I started keeping lists of adoption requests with me during shelter rounds. I figured that, with the high number of animals we impounded daily, statistically I would be able eventually to match the adopter with their sought-after pet.

As I shared in the South Central shelter chapter, I generally would send prospective adopters to this location when they were looking for a cat or kitten. My dear friend and department public relations director, Paul, stopped me one day at our administrative offices and put in a specific animal search request for his friends.

"I have two dear friends that were recently married and live in the Santa Monica area, and they are looking to add an adult cat to their family," he started to tell me.

I knew there was probably more, so I waited.

"It doesn't really matter to them what he looks like—no special request on color—and it doesn't matter if it's a male or female." Then he hesitated, and I knew there was going to be one special quality they were looking for that probably wasn't part of the animal's general description. So again I waited...

"Oh and yes, they want to make sure that he is a mouser."

Of course—there was always some special trait specific to each adopter's situation that would seal the adoption deal.

"Seriously?" I responded. How in the world was I going to be able to determine that by looking at cats in our catteries?

"Oh, I am sure you will find one," he responded. "I told them you are the best at picking out animals for people!"

Just great, I thought—no pressure! I added this cat description to my list and really had no idea how I would identify this mouser. Several weeks later, I was doing my regular rounds at the West Valley shelter. I'd finished walking through the kennels and the medical room and was getting ready to stop by the cattery. One of the kennel attendants was still in one of the cat rooms finishing up cleaning cages when I walked in. As I walked by the rows of cages, some cats were directly up front by the cage doors while other more timid creatures preferred to stay at the rear of the cage. As I came to the end of the first row, someone reached out and tapped me on the shoulder. I turned, and it was a black and white tuxedo cat stretching his front limb with all of his might through the cage bars to reach me.

"Hello baby," I said to him as I moved closer.

"That guy is all about the paws," the kennel attendant replied.

He continued to tap at me, but was very gentle and not using his claws. Just at that moment, the kennel attendant was paged and needed in the front lobby so he left the room. All of a sudden, I had a thought. This kitty seemed very tactile. Maybe he had good mousing skills? Since no one was in the room, I took the opportunity to open his cage and get a better feel for his personality. He immediately jumped into my arms. After a short cuddle session, I set him on the floor in the cattery, and within seconds, he bee-lined for the floor drain in the middle of the room. Within five more seconds, he had removed the cover of the drain and was inspecting the plumbing. Yes, my friends, I had found what I thought could be a great mouser!! He had all the characteristics. He was smart, tactile, inquisitive, and eager. I checked out his impound card and noticed that he had been available for several days and was a young adult. I copied into my notebook his impound number and cage number and returned him to his cage (much to his objection). I ran up to the front office and called Paul.

"I have found him!" was my introductory line.

"Found who?" Paul asked.

"The mouser. He's here at West Valley, but your friends better get out here today or tomorrow because he is already available."

"Oh my God, they will be thrilled. I will call them right away."

And that's how it works. I placed many animals this way. When I came into work the following week, Paul stopped me in the hallway and said, "There is no longer a mouse problem, and they absolutely love this cat! How do you do it?"

I didn't want to give up any of my secrets—which actually are just being observant and being in the right place at the right time—so I replied, "It just goes with the territory." I really wanted to say, there's a lot of luck involved!

The One That Got Away

To keep up my high rate of pairing animals with adopters, I had to stay on top of my game by continually monitoring the animal populations at each shelter. The type of dog you might find to adopt out of the West Valley shelter was much different than a dog from the South Central L.A. shelter for example. Many of the dogs brought into West Valley were over 60 pounds in weight because of the rural properties in the area. People enjoyed and had the space to keep large-sized dogs. You would commonly see many purebreds that seemed to be in excellent condition. There was a large number of hunting dogs, German Shorthaired Pointers, Brittany Spaniels, and plenty of Retrievers. If you were interested in adopting a smaller breed dog, you were in luck too. The West Valley shelter housed popular purebreds like Bichon Frise, Chihuahuas, and at least two Cocker Spaniels at all times.

But when I think of West Valley and focus on breeds of dogs found there, one particular dog stands out in my mind. He was a beautiful, red, adult Doberman.

It was one of those days when the West Valley RVT scheduled for duty called in sick, and the second RVT was on vacation, so I was the designated pinch hitter for the day. I arrived at the shelter knowing my first duty would be euthanasias, so I was moving rather slowly from my car in the parking lot to the employee entrance. The ACT assigned to assist the medical staff with euthanasias for the day met me as I entered the animal holding area. We soon crossed paths with the Senior ACT, who let me know he had cross-checked all of the animals scheduled for euthanasia. He assured me that there were no animals that had traceable identification on them, no members of the public who had interest in adopting them, nor any rescue groups that had placed a hold on an animal. As was the case with all six shelters, we would not just be euthanizing the ill and injured animals. There would be healthy, young animals included on the list due to the large number of animals coming in daily and the smaller number of animals adopted or claimed from this finite holding space. That was always the hardest part about this process.

Even if we could hold animals for an infinite time period, awaiting the perfect adopter "match," that too comes with its own set of unique problems. Dogs that are kenneled for long periods of time (I mean over a year or more, which is done in some "No-Kill" facilities) can develop behavioral problems. The term that is used in shelters is that they become "kennel crazy."

Their behavior may be described as just a significant change from their initial, incoming presentation. For example, a friendly animal may become reclusive, not want human attention anymore, and run away and hide when the opportunity for human interaction presents itself. Soon, this animal is no longer a candidate for a traditional adopter. There may be a special person out there that is willing to invest a great deal of time into this animal to try to re-socialize it, but it is not always easy, or expedient, to find just such a person.

Or the behavior change can be more profound and include circling (abnormal repeated chasing of the tail for 10-20 minutes an episode). Other presentations I have seen include raising their heads and snapping their jaws, trying to catch imaginary objects. Many of these behaviors may surface due to boredom and lack of new stimulation, or perhaps they can just be interpreted as bouts of depression. Unfortunately, the time it has taken these dogs to develop these behaviors is usually proportional to expectations for recovery to normal behavior.

Animals that have been exhibiting these behavior changes for short periods of time may have a chance at integrating into a patient adopter's life. If an animal has had months exhibiting this adverse behavior, it may not be as reasonable to believe that he will recover. So, when folks propose that the solution for stopping euthanasia is just to keep dogs in a kennel for months on end, it really is not a very feasible solution when you are considering what's best for the animal.

On this particular morning, I had situated myself in the euthanasia room and got the controlled substance logs, euthanasia solution, and needles and syringes out and ready for use. The ACT was a very good handler and talked to and petted each animal before we euthanized it. Luckily, the West Valley shelter euthanasia list was not even half as long as the daily South L.A. list. We only had about ten dogs to euthanize that day, and most were ill or deemed unadoptable for various reasons.

The ACT had left the room and gone back out to the kennel area to lead in the next dog. I had my back to the door, completing my log on the last animal. I heard the door open and the familiar voice of the ACT and what sounded like a large-sized dog happily playing and carousing with her. I hesitated for a moment and then turned around to face the ACT and the next unfortunate victim. The dog I saw was truly the most beautiful red Doberman I had ever seen. He was in good flesh, and even in the poor lighting of the room we were standing in, I could tell his coloring was vibrant. He must have weighed around 80 pounds, and he had a huge head which he carried in a friendly and quizzical manner. His little stub of a tail was wiggling with delight, and then his entire rear quarters began to move in unison with the stub.

He was so happy to be out of the kennel and just hanging out with us. Then he did it. He turned to the ACT and jumped up on her, placing his front paws on her shoulders so that he was now her height. He looked her right in the face and gave her a huge, wet lick on the cheek. Now mind you, I am very safety conscious and never allow staff to get their face anywhere near the shelter animals because we do not know them well and they don't know us well. I have seen too many injuries to faces (including the nose of a technician being bitten off) that require plastic surgery and cause tremendous emotional trauma. We can calm animals and let them know we care about them, by talking calmly to them and stroking them without putting ourselves at risk for injury. The ACT knew these rules, and she turned her head to look at me with hopeful eyes. I guess you just had to be in the room with us, but the manner in which this dog gently licked her caused us both to melt.

I walked over to the dog, who had now regained his four feet on the ground stance, and he pushed his big head right up against my thighs to give me a thorough hello and request a pat or a stroke. At that moment, I knew it was over, and I placed his huge lower jaw in the palm of my hand and lifted his head to look into those soul-searching eyes. His ears were erect and alert with life. Without looking at the ACT, I asked her if there were any behavior or illness problems with this dog. She quietly responded, "No," and added, "and he's a wonderful dog."

I asked her why Doberman rescue had not come to take this perfect dog. She responded, "We called her, but she has way too many dogs at her place—I think well over a hundred Dobes. I think we (animal control) may have to go out there and investigate soon. She is in way over her head right now."

My hand left the dog's jaw and moved over the top of his head. As my hands had done so many times before, with so many dogs, they found their way behind his ears and provided a soft caress. I used my hands to trace his neck and strong shoulder muscles, thorax and abdomen. I examined his mouth to find shiny white teeth, with very little dental tartar accumulation and estimated his age at around 12-14 months. I cradled his head one last time in my hands and now could look the ACT in the face. I said, "Get this dog out of here. Don't even ask me to euthanize this dog. He gets more time out there."

As I turned around and faced the wall because I could feel the tears filling up in my eyes, I heard the ACT squeal, grab the leash of the dog, and say, "Let's go buddy. You're out of here."

That was it. No more euthanasias today... I just couldn't do it. We had provided enough space for the shelter for that day.

A few minutes later, I walked out into the kennels on the male side and found the stately Doberman. He was kenneled with two other dogs, and the three of them were crowded in that space. But he seemed happy and content. I looked at him and reached both hands through the kennel gate. He obediently placed his head in my hands and closed his eyes as I rubbed him gently. No one else was around, and I quickly told him to stay up at the front of the gate and get the public's attention when they walk by, assessing all of the adoptable dogs today. I remember telling him, you have to sell yourself.

I stayed that day for a few extra hours after the shelter had opened up to the public, interacted with potential adopters, and directed them to this magnificent animal. I had a couple of people say that they would consider him, but no guaranteed adoptions as of yet.

I had to get back downtown, but before I left, I asked all of the kennel staff to try their best to get this big guy adopted. As I was walking out toward the parking lot exit, the ACT who had assisted me earlier ran after me calling my name. I turned around, and she was running to catch up to me. As she got closer to me, she said, "I just wanted to tell you one thing— Thank You." She paused because she knew that, over the past few months, some animal activists had been calling me cruel, inhumane names. Because I was the animal control veterinarian that had to euthanize animals, they had dubbed me "Dr. Death." She added, "Just let someone try to tell me you don't care for these animals." And as quickly as she had appeared, and before I could even respond to her, she had turned and run back for the entrance to the building.

On the drive back to downtown L.A., I went over and over in my head how I could keep this animal. I already had two dogs at home, and one was a large-sized rescue Greyhound. The biggest problem wasn't the size of my house, but the very small size of my yard. I walked my dogs everyday, several times, but three dogs would be a hand full. Oh, but he was so beautiful, and he and I connected. This was the type of feeling I told adopters to look for when they were searching for the perfect pet to adopt. This feeling would tell them that it was a good fit. I tried very hard to put him out of my mind and go about my business for the remainder of the day.

I went home that evening, walked my dogs, and we all snuggled up together on the bed to watch the news prior to turning out the lights. I could close my eyes and see him joining my "crew," but I also wondered where my husband and I would sleep? I again tried to put him out of my mind.

Several days went by before I could get back out to the West Valley shelter as I was needed at other locations. I entered the kennel area and immediately went to the red Doberman's kennel. I called the dogs from the outside portion of the dog run to come inside so that I could see them. They all ran in, but the Doberman wasn't there. I knew that, often times, dogs were moved from kennel to kennel on a daily basis, trying to find a good mixture of dogs that would get along with each other during their stay at the shelter. At that moment, the RVT entered the kennels, and I asked him about the Doberman.

"You know that big, red Doberman that had been here for a while?" I asked over the insistent barking of all of the dogs on the side of the kennel in which we were standing.

He nodded yes. "Did he get adopted?" I demanded.

He looked at me with that familiar, yet unwanted look. "I euthanized him yesterday."

My heart sank. I should have taken that dog. I should have put a hold on him. I should have taken him.

To this day, I can still close my eyes and see that beautiful red Doberman boy with his gentle mannerisms. I can tell you exactly what kennel he was housed in at the West Valley shelter. It can still bring tears to my eyes. Since that encounter, I have always had a special fondness for red Dobermans. In four years with Los Angeles City Animal Control, this was the dog I missed, a relationship I could have had but I didn't act fast enough, even though I had all of the right signals. He was "the one that got away..."

The Best Deal Ever

About a year later, I was conducting rounds at the West Valley shelter, and as I was walking down the main corridor of the dog runs, I saw a large black Lab crossed with Coon Hound. (The shape of his head and ears was quite distinctive for the breed.) Common animal shelter statistics tell us that black dogs are the lowest on the adoption list. This is for no fault of their own. They just don't stand out in the kennel setting like an all white dog, or a dog of mixed colors like black and white, or a red dachshund for example. I noticed him because I saw that he was limping, and on closer examination, I watched him hold up his left rear paw so that he was only bearing weight on three limbs.

He was housed in a kennel with three other very large-sized dogs, and I didn't want him to be seen as weak in their eyes because that could lead to serious trouble for him. Yes, there is even a hierarchy in a kennel run. The weakest animal can be attacked by kennel mates, can be prevented from eating at the food bin, and I have even seen situations where the weakest dog is not allowed a space to lie down and is forced to stand. Dominance and submission can come in many different forms.

I called this guy over to the front of the kennel gate where I was standing, and he slowly approached me. He pushed his massive head against the kennel gate waiting for a gentle hand, and I immediately obliged. I looked up and saw the veterinary technician in the corridor and called him over to the kennel.

"Eric, have you seen this guy limping?" I asked.

"Yes, he came in off the truck limping. I checked him, and it is only a soft tissue injury," he replied.

"He's at the point now where he is non-weight bearing, so let's put him in a cage in the medical room to give him a chance to rest. I don't think he will do well out in the main kennel," I said.

Eric was also a veterinarian from the Philippines, working in the capacity as a licensed veterinary technician at the shelter.

He was smart and accurate with his observations, and always calm and mild-mannered and very easy to work with. He didn't even raise an eyebrow at my request to relocate this dog that probably weighed around 65-70 pounds, even though this was going to create a hardship for the vet techs because the dog would take up the largest cage in the medical room. That size of cage could be used for a bitch with her pups, but luckily there was one available for our limping dog.

We were able to coax the other dogs in the kennel to the outside of the run, and we dropped the guillotine door that separated the kennel into two equal parts so our limper was isolated in the indoor section of the dog run. Now it was safe to open the gate and bring our patient out into the main corridor. The minute he passed the threshold of the kennel door, I knew he was one of those gentle giants. He slowly hobbled right up to me and instantaneously rested his large head against the front of my legs covering both thighs. I slipped a rope lead over his head and slowly lead him out of the kennel corridor and into the medical room to set him up in a cage. As soon as I opened the cage door, he stepped up and into the cage with the slightest encouragement and let out a groan (perhaps a sigh of relief) as he positioned his heavy body in a comfortable lying position.

I examined his cage card, and it indicated that he was already neutered. Eric had also noted that the dog was at least four years old, and his front incisors were worn down, indicating that he probably had been an outdoor dog and engaged in a bit of fence chewing. I told Eric, "I can't believe the owners are not looking for this sweet boy. They even invested money in him to have him neutered."

Eric said, "It's early. He has only been here a few days, so let's see what happens."

Despite his encouraging words, I knew my new friend's clock at the shelter was ticking in double time because he was not a top adoption candidate due to his injury, his large size, and his black color.

It was kind of an unspoken word after my heartbreak over the red Doberman, but I knew whenever I showed a special interest in an animal at any of the shelters, all of my vet techs made a special note of it on the animal's impound card. Eric told me he would monitor him and keep me posted if his owner came in.

Later that week, I got a call from Eric, and he told me that no one had been looking for the Coon Hound cross. He also told me that he was running out of space and he would have to make a decision very soon on this dog. I understood the situation, but I just didn't know if an injured dog that was limping would do well at my house with a very steep staircase.

Three days later, I received my second call from Eric. "Hey Doc, your dog is here waiting for you."

I took a deep breath and told him I would be by to pick him up the next day. I wanted to time the adoption so that I could take him home right after signing the adoption papers, so I arrived in the West Valley parking lot in the late afternoon.

I walked into the medical room, and there was Eric with a brimming smile standing next to my Coon Hound cross. He said, "He's all ready for you, Doc. I even found him a matching collar and leash!"

He didn't tell me, but I knew where the matching set came from. This may appear a bit odd to those of you who don't work at animal control, but if an animal that is euthanized is wearing a nice collar, it is often kept in case a situation arises where it might be useful to another animal. It may seem morbid, but this was actually a very kind gesture from Eric and his way of thanking me for saving a sweet dog and saving him from another heart-breaking euthanasia.

I looked down at my new pet. He was wearing a bright red collar, and he lifted his head when he saw me like he was ready to go. I told Eric that I needed to sign the paperwork up front and I would be right back.

Adoption fees at most agencies are based on the type of species and whether or not an animal has been previously spayed or neutered. For dogs, it is always more expensive to adopt an intact female because spay surgery is more costly than neutering an intact male dog. The lowest adoption fee is assigned to previously altered males or females.

To this day, I have never forgotten the fee I paid to adopt Roody. (Yes, that is what I decided to call him.) Since he was already neutered, I wrote a check for a whopping thirty-five dollars. Even now, if I make a purchase for anything and the total comes up to thirty-five dollars, I always think of Roody—the best deal ever!

I returned to the medical room, Eric put Roody on the leash for me, and Roody practically dragged me to the entrance of the shelter. We walked outside, and he slowed down a bit and walked by my side. I knew we had at least a two hour drive in traffic from Chatsworth to Long Beach, so Roody took a walk in the grass and relieved himself before we walked to my car. I opened the passenger side door, and without a word, Roody jumped right on the front seat and immediately layed down and closed his eyes as if to say, "Please don't ask me to get out of this car."

We started out on the long drive to his new home, and I drove for most of it with my right hand on top of Roody's head as he slept the entire way and barely moved a muscle. When we arrived in Long Beach, I had to introduce him to my Boston Terrier, which wasn't easy for the first 45 minutes, but with a little patience, they were both walking calmly together around the block on their leashes. Roody never growled and remained submissive the entire time, knowing he was entering the home of another dog who was the established leader. They never once fought, they shared tennis balls, and they slept together for the duration of both of their lives.

Not only was Roody the most gentle and appreciative dog I have ever owned, but he had one other special trait. He LOVED kids. We could be walking on one side of the street, and if he saw children walking on the opposite side, he would drag me across the street so he could meet them. It happened all the time. Several houses down the street from where we lived, the neighborhood kids would gather in the front yard and play soccer. If we would walk by while they were playing, the game would officially go into "time out," and everyone would form a circle around Roody, taking turns petting and hugging him. He would instinctively sit, lean in, and close his eyes. This was his heaven.

But my favorite story about Roody occurred during the season when Girl Scout cookies were for sale. Our neighborhood grocery store was in walking distance from our house, and Roody would often accompany my husband and me for the trip to the store. On one particular day, a Girl Scout troop had a table set up at the store entrance with all of their cookie boxes displayed for sale. The Scouts were positioned behind the table trying to engage customers. Roody always got to pick out the box we would buy, and due to his size, he could easily walk up to the table and nudge the cookie variety of his choice.

This time when Roody was making his choice, one of the little Scouts burst into tears, and it was obvious she was terrified of dogs. I held Roody back and told her that this was her chance to get past that fear and meet the most gentle dog she would ever know. Roody patiently waited while the little girl slowly moved toward the front of the table. I told Roody it was okay, and he took two steps toward her, and with his wonderful sense of compassion, he leaned his huge head into her chest and waited for her to wrap her arms around him. Within seconds, she did, and she lowered her head to touch his. With her head still resting on top of Roody, she looked up at me and said, "I love him." And he had worked his magic again, his special gift—that was my Roody.

My angel, Roody, adopted from the West Valley Shelter—gentle giant and lover of all kids!

Chapter Four:
North Central Shelter, Los Angeles, California

Modern Buildings Don't Change the Reality...

The North Central shelter was the most modern shelter (built in the late 1980's), and it had the largest animal holding capacity of all six shelters. This shelter was the closest to downtown Los Angeles where the department's administrative offices (including mine) were located. Famous landmarks surrounding the shelter included China Town, Dodger Stadium, and the Staple Center (home of the world champion L.A. Lakers professional basketball team).

Much of the area around the shelter consisted of steel-bar-protected industrial buildings, strip malls—and yes, doughnut/fast food shops. These strip malls were so close together that if you were driving and trying to locate a business at the same time, you quickly became dizzy with the similarity and frequency of it all. It seemed that the people who waited in large numbers at the bus stops on these streets were tired, defensive, and never looked you in the eye, and a variety of languages could be heard.

One of these bus benches was in front of a gas station that I frequently used to re-fuel my City vehicle. Even though the station was out in the open, it was wise to stay alert and survey the crowd at the bus stop before unlocking and opening the driver's door. I was ready, with my gas card removed from my wallet and in hand. I quietly slipped out of the driver's seat and quickly slid the gas card through the card verification slot. While waiting the precious seconds for the okay to begin fueling, I moved to the rear of the vehicle, unscrewed the gas cap, inserted the nozzle, and got ready to pump.

While I waited, I listened to the constant buzz of my surroundings—the background noises of the busy street, buses moving at a fast pace, cars honking the minute the red light changed to green, and the underlying Spanish conversations of those waiting at the bus bench. The area was a mixture of small business entrepreneurs as well as individuals that were living in poverty.

Once I started fueling the vehicle, I secured the lever on the pump handle to ensure the gas would continue to flow automatically. Then I would get back into the car and wait for my tank to fill up. If I needed to look at papers, or do anything in my car while waiting for the tank to fill that took my eyes off the street and activities around me, I made sure to lock the door. I always took these precautions in this area, and thankfully, I never had any problems.

There were interesting establishments located near the shelter. Directly across the street was a strip club that made evening shifts at the shelter even more dangerous, with questionable clientele entering and leaving the club and frequent visits from the Los Angeles Police Department. On the other hand, there were a few perks to the location as well. Adjacent to the strip club was a large movie production studio/warehouse that was used weekly by the movie industry for filming. They rented a portion of the shelter's parking lot for their equipment and staff whenever they were filming. In an effort to keep a positive relationship with the shelter, they would often share the leftovers from the lunch buffet with shelter employees. Many of these spreads were quite lavish, and we could always be guaranteed fresh fruit, sandwiches, and cookies galore.

The isolated strips of neighborhood surrounding the shelter were of low socioeconomic status and well known for the gangs that resided there. I can remember hearing the distant sound of gun shots when leaving the shelter in the evening. It was interesting that the gangs didn't "tag" the outdoor murals that were painted on two large walls of the animal shelter. These murals were easily seen and accessed from the street. I was told the reason for this was because, at the time the mural was being designed, the manager of the shelter, with the help of the local police, spoke to the gang leaders. They agreed to leave the mural alone if the artist incorporated some representative symbol of each gang (such as gang colors, a seal, etc.) into the very visible mural. It must have worked because those murals remained untouched.

The houses in the neighborhood were small and made of wood, all of a similar design with a small front porch and angled roofs. Some had a patch of grass out front that was usually covered by plastic toys and "Big Wheels." These lay still, awaiting their next use by the children and grandchildren that resided within. Most houses did not have grass, but some form of gravel or dirt covering this front space that was used for parking non-running vehicles with badly dented fenders, peeling paint jobs, and missing tires.

I recall rarely seeing children or adults walking on the sidewalks. It was unheard of to walk a dog in this area. It was just too dangerous, and every local knew better. Most large-sized dogs were left in the backyard as guard dogs, and the only barrier between them and someone walking in the alley behind the house was either a chain link fence or a rotting wooden fence. Neither appeared to be a reliable form of restraint for this size of dog. There were so many stray dogs roaming the streets, and dogs breaking through backyard fences, that if you were walking your dog, an encounter with one of these animals was highly likely, and an unfortunate outcome was imminent. In a head-to-head confrontation, the stray, street-smart dog would attack the pet dog, who would likely suffer painful injuries or even death.

The exterior of the shelter was rather non-descript, yet it gave an underlying message of "No Trespassing." The murals helped to soften it, but with the electronically gated entrance to the rear parking lot, it was hard to dismiss the fact that this building was built to be secure.

The interior of the shelter was quite impressive, yet so large that it was not uncommon for the general public to become easily lost in the maze of corridors and different animal holding areas. It took me weeks to learn the location of all of the special rooms and the numbering sequence for the dog kennels. The shelter had the capacity to hold several hundred dogs and cats, and auxiliary holding space for isolating animals either for disease reasons or due to their dangerous or fractious nature. The area for the dangerous dogs was a separate row of dog kennels accessed by staff through a locked security door. The animals could be observed by the public through glass, but without direct access to them.

There was an outdoor area used to exercise "long-term hold" dogs, of which many were the shelter's responsibility for up to one year. Because these animals were part of either a humane or cruelty case, they were being held as evidence at the shelter during the lengthy court trial, and they couldn't be dispositioned (adopted, returned to owner, or euthanized) until a verdict from the court was passed down. These animals often took up valuable housing space from the stray animals during their prolonged holding periods, which unfortunately resulted in increased euthanasias. But there was no other choice in these cases. The animals under investigation, by law, had to be held. We tried to house them at other private kennel facilities, but understandably, no one wanted the responsibility of caring for dogs that were extremely dangerous to handle. It placed their staff under stress and at risk for injury. It was also common that the owners of these dogs would make attempts to break into the kennels and steal their animals. No privately-owned kennel could be paid enough to endure all of these problems.

The design of the shelter was all-species encompassing, and it included a barn to house horses or other large animals. There were also outdoor-only dog kennels for emergency population overflow purposes. In addition, there was a grassy area that connected to the barn. It allowed horses to obtain minimum exercise during their holding periods. If you looked carefully at the exterior perimeter walls of this grassy enclosure, there were subtle reminders of the hostile environment that lay beyond the gates. Razor wire ran above the stone walls, and the nearby sound walls that edged the I-5 freeway were tagged with violent gang lingo.

An architectural plus for the North Central shelter was an extensive administrative office area. There was extra space, including an office occupied by a volunteer coordinator that handled all six facilities, and an office for the field veterinarian. This shelter was also the only one that had a formal classroom. About once or twice per year, the eight week training academy for newly-hired animal control officers was held in that room. It hosted the lecture portion of the curriculum. Around the corner from the classroom was a vast warehouse where supplies like gloves, boots, officer's equipment, and animal traps were kept and distributed to the remaining five locations. In back, a secured parking lot garaged the animal control vehicles, including horse trailers. It was also utilized to store emergency city vehicles from a number of other departments. It wouldn't be uncommon to see police and fire vehicles parked there as well as large trailers.

Because this facility had so much extra space and was located centrally in the city, most department press conferences and special programs were scheduled at this shelter. It was essential, with the high number of activities passing through these doors, that the kennel and medical staff were not only dependable, but willing to put in extra time to ensure activities and events flowed smoothly.

Vince—Hiring a Great RVT

Recently after my appointment as Chief Veterinarian, I participated in interviews to permanently fill several RVT positions as well as the Senior ACT position at the North Central shelter.

As I have explained earlier, many of my current RVTs were Philippino veterinarians that were not yet licensed to practice in the United States so they were working in the capacity as licensed veterinary technicians. They were a close-knit group of very qualified and team-oriented staff. Whenever I had the opportunity to hire additional RVTs, I didn't hesitate to get their recommendations for former veterinary classmates that might be looking for work. As a result, I had several RVT temporary hires that were waiting for the city's Human Resource

Department to conduct an exam for the position so they could become permanent hires. The exam consisted of a written section and a preliminary interview. How a candidate performed on both parts of the exam determined their ranking on the list of possible hires. Candidates were asked to come in for final interviews starting with those who ranked highest on the list.

For the first round of interviews, there was a cut off for the ten top candidates, so it was important for applicants to do well on this exam. When the list arrived at my desk, I scanned it quickly to identify where in the ranking my temporary hires were placed since I knew I wanted them hired as permanent employees. I found almost all of my RVT temporary employees in the top five, but one was conspicuously absent, my current lead RVT from the North Central shelter. How could that be? He was exceptionally qualified and certainly one of the top RVTs in the department. I looked a bit further down the list and still didn't find him. I looked even farther until I finally found his name. My heart sank. I would have to get through about ten candidates, not including his fellow temporary staff buddies, before I could reach him for an interview. I reviewed his exam results and saw that he had performed poorly on the interview portion. I was not about to lose him, so I knew I needed a strategy to make this happen.

I brought in three of my temporary hires for the final interview, they did well, and I was able to put them on the permanent list. I went to the North Central shelter and explained the situation to Vince. As I spoke, I remember his head was tilted downward. Looking at the floor, he said, "Doc, I am so sorry I let you down. I got really nervous during the interview, and I knew I didn't do well. Just let me know when I need to pack my bags."

I made him look me straight in the eye and said, "I don't want to hear that. I will figure this out, but you need to give me a little time."

I knew he had a family and that he was studying for the foreign veterinary accreditation exams so he could practice veterinary medicine in the U.S. There should always be an answer for every problem, right? I went over and over several options, but none of them seemed reasonable. Then I came up with the easiest solution. I needed to stall the hiring process. I stalled, then I stalled some more, then a little more. I stopped interviewing candidates and weeks went by. I claimed my schedule was so packed with field work that I couldn't get the interviews in. The department's human resource representative paid me weekly visits at my administrative office trying to pin me down for interview dates. He would also bring in the updated RVT list. Over time, other candidates would drop off the list because they would find other employment. Gradually the list was getting smaller, and my hope was that eventually Vince would rise on the list so that I could bring him in for an interview.

One day the General Manager for the department caught me in the hallway and instructionally said, "Doctor, you need to finish hiring those RVTs."

My response was, "Busy, sorry, gotta go, but I am getting to it. Don't worry!"

Every day that I did rounds at the North Central shelter during that period of time, when Vince was on duty, he would meet me in the medical room and say, "Doc, is today the day that you send me home?"

I finally told him to knock it off. I was not going to lose him. He just had to trust me.

Then one fine day over a month after the initial list was generated, Vince ranked at a level where I could bring him in for an interview. I was elated. During the interview, we asked him questions about general animal care, shelter-related duties, and policies and procedures. Vince answered the questions, but in as short an answer as possible. After he responded, I would have to say things like, "Anything else you would like to add? Could you elaborate on that for me?" This was my best effort to get him to relay to the panel all of his knowledge and expertise. I can see why he struggled in the first interview.

Finally it was over, and I had secured all of my temporary RVTs, including Vince. I know Vince was so grateful, not only to be permanently hired, but because eliminating the stress he was enduring throughout this lengthy process must have been like lifting a 50 pound weight from his shoulders. All of the staff (especially me and the animals also) let out a big sigh of relief when they knew Vince would still be on board at North Central.

Brea—Hiring a Great ACT Supervisor

For the ACT Supervisor position at North Central, there were many qualified candidates, but I was also looking for someone with high energy, loyalty to the department, and an eagerness to take a chance in new and exciting events I hoped we'd be able to put together. I didn't have to look far. I knew I had found her when I interviewed Brea. She was very committed to her work and took pride in the North Central shelter, where she was currently the acting Senior ACT. This is where I came to know Brea.

Brea was a young Hispanic woman with thick, wavy auburn hair. She always wore her hair high on the top of her head fastened with a large hair clip so that it fanned out behind her like a huge tail. She stood about five feet, three inches, tall and had recently given birth to her second son. She was very physically involved with her work and helped her staff haul heavy, high-powered hoses throughout the kennels to clean the individual dog runs. She frequently could be found assisting with unloading pallets as well. The pallets held 50-pound sacks of dry dog food and cases of canned dog and cat food! Through all of this, I noticed that she took her shoes off in her office whenever possible and complained of aching feet. She frequently colored her hair an auburn/red because someone had told her that it would hide the freckles she so despised. Her freckles were precisely placed all over her cheeks and nose. I tried to tell her that those freckles made her very attractive and unique—even fun-loving—but she just wouldn't hear of it.

Initially, she was very business-like with me, but as I got to know her, I was able to get her to smile and laugh, and I discovered a woman with individuality and a goal for high achievement. In addition to her newborn son, she was also raising a young boy just starting high school. He was very bright, wonderfully polite, and had her special smile. He volunteered at the shelter quite a bit and was always dependable, just like his mother. I understood that Brea had learned through her childhood how to be a survivor, no matter what it took. I saw many positive attributes in Brea that would serve the shelters and animals well, so I trusted her. I hoped that, if she could sense the confidence and trust I had in her, she would succeed and not have to spin her wheels as much, worrying about surviving.

She had proven to me on many occasions over the past few months that she was my "go-to gal" and could complete any assignment I gave her. She knew the North Central shelter backwards and forwards. Her animal records were always accurate. She checked and checked again the status of animals prior to euthanasia, to ensure no mistakes were made. The RVTs depended on her, were confident working with her, and trusted her organizational skills. Even though she worked the day shift, she was known to come into the shelter periodically during the swing and graveyard shifts to monitor her staff. She took her own time to train new kennel staff personally for all three shifts so that they would be qualified to work anytime at all six locations. Taking all of this into consideration, I moved forward with her appointment to the permanent position of Senior ACT.

Many people, once they obtain a promotion, throttle back a bit and don't work as hard because they have achieved their goal of filling the new position. But not Brea... From that moment on, she never wavered, slacked off, or took her responsibilities for granted. I saw a new sparkle in her eye. She had just received the pat on the back she so richly deserved, and it acted to motivate and inspire her.

Brea soon became my key "extra activity foundation," showing excellent organizational skills and dependability. Not only was she strategically located near my office and most city activities, but she was there for me after hours, on weekends—just whatever it took.

Brea took control of one of the extra programs—promoting adoptions from the shelters. She coordinated the weekly television morning news segment, "Pet of the Week," with the most popular morning news channel in the city of Los Angeles, KTLA. This task was in addition to her regular workload of caring for well over 200 animals daily, and monitoring her staff on 24 hour shifts. Every week, the day prior to our weekly program, she took the time to walk through the North Central kennels and cattery to find a dog and a cat that would be suitable to take on television. This was by no means an easy task.

There were six main corridors of dog kennels, which housed anywhere from two to five dogs per enclosure. Fortunately for the animals, these kennels were state of the art. They contained an indoor and outdoor section divided by a guillotine door that was manually operated from the outside of the kennel. This door provided the ability to cordon off animals from each other if a fight broke out, as well as to segregate animals on one side during cleaning, sanitizing, and drying of the kennel on the flip side. So the kennels were roomy, safe, and easily sanitized. Despite all of these so-called "luxuries"—it came down to the main issue of too many animals and never enough kennel space.

The males were isolated in one section of corridors and the females in another section. The main reason for segregating these animals based on their sex is that the vast majority of stray animals that are impounded are not spayed or neutered and are able to breed. If they were not segregated, it would become a breeding festival and simultaneously a battleground of dog fighting.

The minute any person walked down one of these aisles, it would stimulate the inhabitants of each kennel run to "come alive." The sociable dogs would rocket to the front of the kennel gate and madly work to get the person's attention. That meant behaviors ranging from barking and whining, to jumping up and down against the kennel gate with wet (sometimes urine-soaked) paws. The latter was the best attention getter as the person wiped the moisture from his or her cheek, wondering what the origin of the liquid really was. The quiet, more-subdued animals would either stay behind their rambunctious kennel mates or be found huddling in the far corners of the kennel. Many times, a person was looking for just such a heartbreaking little face because that was the one who would be snatched up for adoption.

With all of this physical activity and the noise factor, it was very difficult, even for an experienced animal assessor like Brea, to evaluate an animal's appearance and personality. Choosing just one dog for the Pet of the Week segment was also a troublesome decision for the selector because it meant that each animal not chosen would have an uncertain fate. It was a tremendous responsibility to undertake, considering that not choosing an animal might result in that animal being scheduled for euthanasia days later if no one showed interest in adopting it. Sadly, it may be true that the only reason there is no interest in an animal is that he/she did not receive the proper publicity or wasn't in the right place at the right time. And that opportunity may be missed for an animal if they are not chosen for special programs like the KTLA Morning News show.

Brea always had a good mental inventory of the individual animals that she was housing in her shelter on any given day. She was very similar to many of the other employees in that she too had her favorite animals, the ones that pulled at her heartstrings. But in addition to picking an adorable dog, she also had to be sure that the dog would tolerate being held for 5-10 minutes at a time while on the show. Some dogs just don't like to be held, cuddled, or fussed with. They just want to be a dog and keep all four feet on the ground. That's okay, but they wouldn't meet the criteria for appearing on the Morning News show.

Since a cat was also chosen to appear weekly with a dog on the show, Brea evaluated the cats to determine what their tolerance level would be when positioned near a dog. I recall an amazingly complaisant adult female cat that was scheduled to appear on the show with a very rambunctious young puppy. While Brea and I waited in the green room at the television studio with both animals prior to our taping, the puppy played with every studio employee who came in, and he tried relentlessly to get this adult cat to play with him too. Finally, after about a half an hour, he just couldn't do it anymore and collapsed from exhaustion. Brea was seated on a sofa in the green room with the cat resting comfortably, half its body on the sofa and the other half resting on Brea's chest. It seemed a perfect place for a cat that was in charge to be residing. The compelling part of this picture was that the puppy, who had succumbed to exhaustion from his gallivanting, huddled around the kitty's belly with his head resting on her side, submerged in her soft haircoat, his eyes closed and in a deep slumber. The cat didn't budge and continued to appear content, cuddling with Brea and her new puppy sibling. I looked at Brea and, part in jest and part seriously, I said, "You really have a gift for picking these guys. Did you plan this?"

She gave me that coy look, rolling her eyes, and just continued to stroke the kitty, who responded with a deep purr that filled the green room.

The TV Gig and the Sleep Over

The day before the show, Brea made sure the animals were bathed by the ACT on swing shift (4:00 P.M.—midnight) and housed separately from other animals so they stayed clean for the next morning. She arranged on the day of the show to have either one of her ACT staff or herself, if she was short-staffed, transport the animals to the studio by 7:30 A.M. In the three straight years that we were fortunate enough to keep the "gig" with KTLA, she never transported the wrong animal, never had an animal transported late, and never brought an unbathed animal. As you may have gathered, the process of choosing and transporting an animal for a television show is complicated and time-consuming.

So that Brea could take a break from the pressure of choosing animals each week, we tried to identify animals from the other five shelters, rotating the animal celebrities of the week. That really took some coordination. I depended on my staff at each shelter to alert me to animals they thought would be good candidates for the show. Each shelter always had a "special" animal that they all desperately wanted to see adopted. When they called me in advance about a particular animal, I would usually set up my day to come by that shelter the day before the morning show, do my rounds, then load up the animals for transport to the North Central shelter.

Because of the horrendous L.A. commuter traffic in the mornings, it was impossible to transport animals to the television station from other shelters besides North Central. We tried doing this only once, and we discovered that we would have to leave the shelters at 5:30 A.M. to ensure our 7:30 A.M. arrival, and that was just ludicrous. Our days were already long enough. So we developed this system of transporting animals from the other shelters to the North Central shelter under Brea's supervision, the day before the taping. The animals would spend the night there, be ready for transport to the studio in the morning, and after I finished the taping, I would load them up in my city vehicle and transport them back to the shelter of origin. I fondly called this adventure the "sleep over."

I always respected Brea and would not think of bringing additional animals to her shelter without informing her first. Whenever I would call Brea and ask her if I could bring some animals over for the "sleep over," she would pause on the phone, and I'd know she was rolling her eyes, scrunching up her nose to obliterate the freckles there. But she knew exactly what I needed and always made space for them. Brea came to expect my phone calls the day before the television taping, and before I could even get the words out, she would say, "Who's coming for the sleep over?"

As kennel supervisor for the North Central shelter, Brea served as designated morning transporter to the show on probably more occasions than she would prefer to remember. She was always at the studio before I was, and I would find her waiting in the lobby with two cuddly creatures. Many times before I got there, the behind the scenes television crew would have confiscated both animals and would have them in the makeup room where everyone would take turns cuddling with them. The idea behind bringing animals on the morning show was not only to facilitate the adoption of that animal, but to create awareness with the public about the wonderful animals that can be found at the animal control shelter.

I also took the opportunity to discuss the topic of responsible pet ownership at each appearance. Sometimes we talked about caring for a puppy or kitten. Sometimes we described how to handle a pet behavior problem. And we discussed common illnesses in pets. The format was so successful that, ultimately, the show devoted a segment of their website to the "Pet of the Week" program. Folks could send in an e-mail question for Dr. Dena that would be answered on the air. It was great fun and helpful to me to understand what issues were of greatest concern to the public.

Often times, we would have to wait past our designated airtime because a special news report or traffic problem delayed our portion of the show. We didn't mind. We just sat in the green room and played with our soon-to-be animal television stars and enjoyed meeting the celebrities that were guests on the morning show. Most celebrities stopped to pet each of the animals before they went either into the make-up room or on air for their interviews. Some of them, I never would have recognized without their make-up applied by experts. Brea and I had a ball poking fun at their individual idiosyncrasies and watching their "performances." As we saw, it was not uncommon for celebrities to "get their way." This extended to the animals we brought for the show. Several of the celebrities fell hopelessly in love with some of these animals and just "had to have them."

I have to say that we did not play favorites. We made each one of them go through the same process that an ordinary member of the public did if they were interested in adopting the animal featured on the Pet of the Week program. We would receive sometimes up to 20 phone calls from interested adopters who were watching the show at home. We'd get these calls almost immediately after we went off the air with the animal featured that day. Some folks called from cities up to 50 miles away from the shelter. Many people responded from an impulse to reach out to an adorable cuddly creature, but when the time came to actually adopt the animal, many folks couldn't make the final commitment. So for that reason, we developed the policy that the interested adopter must come down to the shelter if they really wanted the animal. Of course, the celebrities didn't have time to come to the shelter, so they sent their publicist or their assistants, but they did follow the rules, pay the adoption fees, and wait for the animals to be spayed or neutered. I always believed that celebrity or not, we are all people and I believed in treating people equally.

Celebrity Adoptions

I specifically recall three celebrities/adopters that fell desperately in love with one of our beloved shelter pets featured on the morning news with KTLA.

The first one was Kyra Sedgwick who was a guest on the show promoting her new movie with John Travolta. The dog of the day came from the West Los Angeles shelter and was a small, adorable Shih Tzu. This little ball of fluff was perfect for a sexy actress, and Ms. Sedgwick just had to have her. After the taping of the show, she sent her assistant to the shelter to pay the fees for the dog, and we sent the dog to a private veterinarian for sterilization.

The following night, Ms. Sedgwick had an appearance on the Tonight Show with Jay Leno. She was so excited to have adopted this little dog that, during her introduction on the show, she appeared holding the little dog close to her face and proudly announced that she'd adopted her from the shelter. The young dog was already a professional and seemed to smile for the camera. Her little black button eyes were shining, and she let just a trace of her pink tongue peak through her partially separated lips. This was a great national endorsement for shelter dogs everywhere. Even famous movie stars find lifelong pets at shelters. When Mr. Leno was interviewing Ms. Sedgwick, he couldn't help but make fun of this totally "girly" dog (based on her fluffy, toy-like appearance) and wondered how Ms. Sedgwick's actor husband, Kevin Bacon, would look walking this little dog down the street. Ms. Sedgwick didn't seem to care. She was too enthralled with her new addition to the family.

Another "famous" adoption involved renowned actor Tony Curtis. While Mr. Curtis was preparing for his morning interview on the KTLA Morning News Show, he had to deal with comments from the young camera staff who asked if he was Jamie Lee Curtis' dad. Indeed, Mr. Curtis was getting on in years, but he still had the charisma and high energy that was his trademark during his era in Hollywood. Different from Ms. Sedgwick's choice of a perfect pet, Mr. Curtis' animal interest was in a young cat we were featuring on the show. This male kitty was unusually marked with a glorious silver and black striping along his back and sides. It made him look exotic indeed. He had a unique personality to match and absolutely loved to be handled. You could hear him purring from across the room while he laid stretched out in a fancier's arms. When Mr. Curtis saw him, he became infatuated with him. Mr. Curtis was so taken by this cat that he asked to be part of the Pet of the Week segment taping in addition to his interview, and I was honored to appear on television with him.

During the taping, the adventurous kitten jumped on his shoulder and proceeded to walk along the back of his neck, back and forth, from shoulder to shoulder, brushing the occasional tail under Mr. Curtis' nose, which added to the entertainment of it all. It was obvious that Mr. Curtis was astute in handling cats as he held this kitty and caressed him throughout the show. I spoke to Mr. Curtis after the taping, and he told me that, if no one called about the cat to adopt it, he would definitely take it. His assistant approached me and told me that, at Mr. Curtis' home, he had four other purebred cats that slept on his pillow with him at night, so I need not worry that the cat would have a wonderfully spoiled life ahead of him. That was very comforting to know. It is often difficult working at a shelter—not really knowing, despite the level of screening that you do on adopters, what types of lives await the animals you are giving them. But in this case, I was confident that the kitten "pauper" was soon to become a handsome "prince."

Brea and I took the kitten back to the North Central shelter, and amazingly enough, no one came in to adopt this youngster. I contacted Mr. Curtis' agent, and he was delighted that the kitty would soon be coming to live at the Curtis mansion in Beverly Hills. We wanted this to be extra special, so Brea offered to deliver the kitten. (I suspect that she had an underlying motive to get a glimpse of the mansion as well.) Brea took her work seriously as always and bathed the little kitten. She also purchased a brand new carrier for transport and a mess of toys for the little guy. When I came by to make sure the now-neutered kitten was healthy and ready to go, I found him playing in Brea's office among all of his new toys. Brea was sitting at her desk doing some paperwork and keeping one eye on the kitten to make sure he stayed out of trouble. I smiled and nonchalantly said, "Well, I guess he's ready for his new life."

She looked up and said, "Yes, we should all be so lucky." With that, she picked up the little guy, gave him a gentle kiss on the forehead, loaded him into his carrier with his toys, and they were off. Unfortunately, she only got as far as the entry of the house (no grand tour) and spoke with the assistant, but she commented that there was no doubt in her mind that the kitten would be just fine.

About a week later, I received a phone call from Mr. Curtis himself. He told me that he spent a great deal of money on the other purebred cats that he owned, but this little stray kitten had the best personality of all of them. Every night, this little guy could be found lying on the pillow right next to Mr. Curtis' head, purring his way to sleep. I thanked him for supporting our shelters, and he in turn offered his assistance in the future. A few days later, I received in the mail an autographed picture of a much younger Tony Curtis, and I added it to my celebrity photo wall in my office. Working in Los Angeles, I frequently came in contact with many celebrities on the KTLA Morning News show, through my appearance on the LEEZA talk show, and working on local promotions with celebrity animal advocates. I have a handsome collection of autographed photographs. But this autograph from Tony Curtis was a favorite because it had a great adoption story behind it.

The third celebrity adoption I want to tell you about involved actress Jacqueline Bisset. She had starred in many films, but she was famous for her appearance in the movie, "The Deep." She was a guest on the KTLA morning news program promoting her most recent film. That particular day, we had a young Airedale cross from the Harbor shelter as the featured Pet of the Week. Ms. Bisset was absolutely drawn to this scruffy little black and tan cutie pie. (Scruffy dogs are one of my favorites too.) She almost missed her queue for her interview because she was spending time with us, holding the dog, and learning everything she could about him. After he went on the air, she told me that she just must have him. I explained the rules for adoption, and she became increasingly more stressed and concerned about finding the shelter, which freeway to take, etc. It was always interesting to interact with some of these celebrities who found it very difficult to take on everyday tasks, like driving for themselves. They were totally dependent on their staff of drivers, wardrobe, and fitness folks.

Ms. Bisset's assistant was the nicest man. He basically told her he would handle everything, as I assumed was status quo. I worked with him exclusively, and he told me that his partner would come to the shelter when we opened that day and pay the fees for the dog. Then he pulled me aside and told me he had a plan. Ms. Bisset was supposed to do an evening taping on another talk show in Los Angeles that very night, which also was her birthday. He knew they couldn't permanently have the dog yet because it was scheduled to be neutered the next day, but he wondered if I would bring the dog to the taping and surprise her and appear on the show with her. Then I would take the dog back to the shelter for the night, he would go for surgery in the morning, and then he'd be taken to Ms. Bisset's Los Angeles home. Of course I agreed. Miss out on an opportunity to advertise shelter animals on a national talk show—and appear with Jacqueline Bisset? Are you crazy?

The whole thing was rather complicated, and it took me about two hours to transport the dog through the evening commuter traffic from the shelter to the studio in the East Valley area. When I arrived, the television crew quickly shuffled me off into hiding in the blue room. There the little dog and I waited for our surprise entry onto the set.

A few minutes before Ms. Bisset was introduced to the audience, I was maneuvered to the far end of the set, off camera. The talk show host thanked Ms. Bisset for appearing on the show and announced that it was her birthday. He said that he had a special birthday present for her. That was my queue. I walked onto the set with this little scruffy guy in my arms, and Ms. Bisset jumped up, and with unbelieving eyes, looked at the host and proudly announced that this was the dog she'd just adopted earlier today. It was a wonderful five minutes of interactive dialogue between the host, Ms. Bisset, and myself about shelter animals and the importance of spaying and neutering pets to control pet overpopulation at your local shelter. Ms. Bisset was a true believer in helping these animals, and I complemented her repeatedly for "doing her part." She had saved a life today. During the entire interview, she held the pup close to her cheek as he calmly sat in her lap.

About three years later, a friend of mine sent me in the mail a copy of a small animal-interest magazine that had Jacqueline Bisset on its cover. In the photograph, sitting next to her in the backyard of her Los Angeles home, was the now-adult Airedale cross, just as scruffy as ever. The article spoke of her admiration for this special little dog that she'd adopted from the local animal shelter after seeing him on a morning news program. This too was what I call a good fit and a permanent adoption placement. These experiences were definitely the "perks" of being involved in such a large sheltering agency in the fast-moving city of Los Angeles.

Vaccination Clinics

Appearing on television was only a small part of reaching out to the public that we worked with every single day. Even though Los Angeles may be the home of "the beautiful people" and places from the movie and television industry, the vast majority of its inhabitants do not live that life, and they need assistance from public agencies like animal control. One of the most challenging programs that we put together for the public was our vaccination clinics. We identified areas of the community that were in need of support and provided free vaccinations and licensing of their dogs. The whole process of setting up a massive vaccination clinic was cumbersome. The clinics operated on Saturdays from 8:00 A.M. to noon, and staff ran the entire operation, except for the police protection. Many of the supplies we utilized, like needles and syringes, made our events prime targets for certain people. Add to that the fact that the clinics were set up in needy areas, which unfortunately contained gangs and drug users, and it was mandatory that we have a protective police presence.

When deciding where in the community the event would take place, it was necessary for us to travel to proposed sites. The sites were often neighborhood recreation centers or parks that were well known and easily accessible to that particular community. We had to coordinate dates and times with the staff of the facilities to ensure we weren't overlapping activities like local basketball or baseball tournaments. Since each park and center was physically laid out differently, we walked the premises and decided how we would set up the assembly line. We needed to determine where animals would be lined up with their owners and how we could keep them in the shade and their paws off the hot asphalt. Tables needed to be strategically set up to ensure money was collected for dog licenses before owners had a chance to get vaccinations for their pets and slip out without paying the license fee. Once that was decided, we needed to coordinate distribution of flyers to the area to announce the clinic. So this process started months before the actual clinic was in operation. I participated in many clinics located at community sites, but we also conducted one of our largest events in the front parking lot of the North Central shelter.

This particular vaccination clinic event was coupled with the opening of an on-site low-cost spay/neuter clinic for performing sterilization surgeries on adopted shelter animals and pets owned by the public. This service was contracted to an out-of-state company. So, in addition to free vaccinations at the L.A. event, we also gave out coupons for spaying and neutering, which resulted in large crowds of anxious people showing up with their pets.

Our event began at 9:00 A.M., but by 8:00 A.M. we had over 100 people standing in line. They had come with their dogs on leashes and their cats in carriers, and in addition to their pets, most of these people had two to four young children standing with them.

Crowd control and management of the animals was our first and probably most challenging endeavor for the day. Dogs of all sizes and temperaments were present. Owners came with various degrees of animal handling experience, purpose, and attention spans. The majority of the people were there to have their animals vaccinated. Some of the animals were adults that had never been on the end of a leash before and had never left the backyard of their owner's home, where they lived day in and day out. Many of the leashes and control devices were homemade. They were made from rope, electrical wire, and one owner had even rigged up a steel pole to serve as a primitive rabies pole like those used by animal control to handle biting and fractious animals. But not all of the people were there because they wanted their pets vaccinated.

A few young boys had decided to bring the toughest pit bulls from their backyards to see if they could create hysteria throughout the lines of people, or to watch their dog start (and finish) a fight with an unsuspecting pet. This was not our first vaccination clinic, and we had expected a select few people to engage in this type of irresponsible behavior—so we were ready for them.

Monica—the Master Dog-handler

I had one special ACT specifically assigned to the duty of monitoring difficult dogs and humans, and her name was Monica. She was a rugged Hispanic woman, solid and tenacious. She had been an ACT for over 10 years and was one of the best dangerous animal handlers that I have ever seen. It was so important for kennel staff working in the L.A. shelters to become expert rope handlers. A large portion of the animals that come into the shelter could be rated from difficult to dangerous to handle.

Monica was a first-rate roper and made an art out of placing a rope around a dog's neck and muzzle. The key to roping an unpredictable dog was to exude confidence and not hesitate when placing the rope. Monica could place a rope around the neck of a dog in the form of a collar and then, using the same rope, without getting her hands anywhere near the nose and mouth of the dog, snap the rope around the dog's muzzle with a slip knot and gain full control of the animal. She performed this exercise in one fluid motion. The dog didn't even know what happened to it and didn't have a chance to become stressed or react in an aggressive manner. Most dogs once muzzled in this way immediately became submissive and calm, knowing that the control of the situation was in the hands of the person at the end of the rope. In many situations at the shelter, and on the streets, this was the best and the only way to handle these animals safely and humanely.

Monica was also regularly called upon to handle the most difficult and fractious dogs in the shelter. Throughout her career, which spread over 15 years, she was never bitten—not once!! She was never rough with dogs. She never got frustrated or lost her cool. She understood them. She was patient, always considered safety in every situation, and respected every animal that came across her path. I felt that I had seen some aggressive dogs through my work as a technician in my early teens and through veterinary school, but I could never have imagined the type of dogs I saw in our quarantine section—dogs who had bitten a person and were under a 10-day rabies quarantine for observation.

I walked through the quarantine areas on a regular basis at all of the shelters. So did the county veterinarians from public health who came through and checked on these dogs and officially released them from quarantine. A high percentage of these dogs were pit bulls or pit crosses that weighed between 90-110 pounds. Many were designated as "guard dogs" and had little-to-no human contact. Their owners kept them for security reasons and released them at night to walk the fence line and patrol junk yards, tire shops, or other similar business establishments in the roughest areas of the city. They were worth their weight in gold to these proprietors because, if a potential intruder saw them, that's all it would take to discourage him from trespassing on the property. These dogs ended up in quarantine when the occasional "not so bright" criminal would underestimate their agility and strength, would take the chance of breaking and entering, and would get bitten—or some unforeseen circumstance occurred and the dog got out or came in contact with a stranger resulting in a bite.

Regardless of temperament, quarantine dogs had to be handled in the shelter on a daily basis during feeding, watering, and kennel cleaning. At the older facilities, the kennel runs weren't constructed so that animals could be isolated on one side of the run without employee contact during cleaning. Instead, dogs had to be manually removed from the kennel and relocated so that their housing area could be cleaned and sanitized. Moving these dogs was not so much a test of strength as it was an exercise in developing a confident and safe approach upon entry (as well as an escape plan if the situation went south). One also needed the ability to handle the Rabies Pole. Monica was an expert in these situations, and I am positive that many kennel attendants were saved from injury by following her lead and adopting her methods.

It is no surprise that I took Monica with me on community vaccination clinic days. There was no doubt that she could handle and protect everyone from any disorderly dog we might encounter on that day. Monica seemed to maintain the level of confidence and calm needed in a stressful situation like handling a vicious dog by concentrating on the animal. But sometimes she forgot to take notice of the owner, or she treated the owner with the same tone as she treated the dog. This created problems in our public relations effort, especially with people who owned trouble-making animals. Such people usually come to these events with a chip on their shoulders. So I tried to keep one eye out to help Monica with the "people" part of the assignment, and I just stayed out of her way during the "control of the animal" part.

Monica's assignment was to monitor the owner and pet line, as well as the outer portion of the shelter property to watch for large sized dogs that were approaching. If any dog looked unruly or like the owner could not handle it, Monica pulled them from the vaccination line and took them to a remote corner of the shelter property. She would then call for a vaccinator to come out to her and the dog. There she would provide restraint, the vaccine would be given, the license fees would be paid for, and the dog and owner would be sent on their way. Even though pet owners spend time with their pets and feel they know them, we never allowed an owner to restrain their pet during our clinics. Many owners didn't realize that their dog was now out of his comfortable environment at home and was faced with the sight and smell of over a hundred unfamiliar and at times unfriendly dogs. These conditions were certainly enough to make a dog uncomfortable. Dogs might act out of character and possibly even turn on their owners if they felt endangered.

For that reason, my staff took responsibility for the restraint of each animal at the clinic. I can confidently report that we never had even one animal or human injury. Monica contributed greatly to this success rate. As a matter of fact, she took her responsibility so seriously that I remember one instance where Monica saved the day and averted certain disaster when a gang member at the vaccination clinic brought his three Bull Mastiffs for display, and "supposedly" for vaccinations.

Toughest Dog on the Block

I happened to be working the front of the line, administering vaccinations with my RVT staff, when several little girls around eight years old who were in line with their pets let out a terrified scream and simultaneously jumped from the ground to the table top where animals were being examined. Before I could even ask them what was wrong, they screamed the name of a dog and pointed to the perimeter of the shelter property. As I looked up, I saw a teenage boy and probable gang member with the largest female Bull Mastiff that I had seen in a long time. She was aggressively tugging like crazy on the end of her lead, which was attached to her reverse-spiked collar. She was hypersalivating, totally focused on the first fifty small and toy breed dogs that were lined up ahead of her. To top that off, the teenager had two other younger Mastiffs on leashes in his other hand. All were equally out of control. The rest of the incident seems to have happened in slow motion.

I remember calling out for Monica, to draw her attention to the three dogs. Of course, she had already seen them and was quickly making her way over to that part of the property. As I watched helplessly from the front of the vaccination line, I got a clear view of the teenage dog owner, who was acting like he could no longer hang on to the large, lunging female. My glance swept over the animals in line that were near this dog, and my heart sank because most of them were small dogs with unsuspecting owners. I looked up one final time to see the young boy let go of the leash. The huge Mastiff, now free, was bee-lining directly for the small dogs in the line. Out of the corner of my eye, I saw Monica. She came out of nowhere, and through the commotion, I saw her running directly for the dog, head on. As her path intersected that of this 150-pound Mastiff, they both traversed a grassy area that had standing water in it. All I could see was Monica diving for the head of the dog because water cascaded up from the puddle and obliterated the view I had of the two of them.

As quickly as the water had sprayed up, it settled again, and there was Monica, scrambling to her feet with her rope lead securely around the neck of the dog, using all of her strength to drag this dog away from the animals in line and back to the owner. The dog owners in the crowd cheered Monica, who was covered from head to toe in mud. I closed my eyes, took a deep breath, and let out a sigh of relief. My mind played tricks on me as I began to picture the shaken and torn bodies of many beloved pets. Monica had prevented all of this from happening and proved once again that she was truly the most skilled animal handler I had ever seen in action.

As for the little girls that had jumped on the vaccination tables prior to the release of the Mastiff, I helped them down and they still looked terrified. They looked at me and said, "You don't know. That's Molly, and she is the meanest dog in our neighborhood. She would have killed all of us."

I had to stop vaccinating for a few minutes and try to understand the terror these small children must go through daily, living in a neighborhood of dangerous dogs. They must wonder every day whether or not these dogs have gotten out of their yards. Are they running loose? Will children be attacked playing in their front yards or walking to school?

Throughout Los Angeles, there were gang members and others who owned dogs primarily for macho reasons. To have the toughest dog on the block, to make money off of backyard dog fighting, to breed the meanest dog and make money off of the sale of the pups... There just were not enough animal control officers to respond to all of the public's complaints about these animals—animals that had the potential to become public safety concerns—injuring or even killing an unsuspecting son, daughter, grandchild, or elderly person. The new trend for gang members was to use their pit bull-type dogs to intimidate or injure other gang members in order to rule the streets. It had become a terrifying reality—a reality in which many innocent bystanders became the bloody victims.

Animal Control agencies throughout the country handle dangerous dog cases. Their investigations include files filled with photographs of severely and permanently disfigured young children and adults. It is not uncommon for the small children who are attacked to loose an ear or their nose during these attacks. Many of the adults end up with deep lacerations to their arms and hands—some with permanent nerve damage and other attacks resulting in the loss of fingers. One case I was told about by the officers involved an older man who was attacked on the street, and to this day, he remains in a vegetative state with only his young daughter to take care of him. He is unaware of and unresponsive to his surroundings. I soon realized that vicious dogs were like loaded weapons.

Whenever a dog involved in a vicious attack on a person was impounded into the shelter and the owner requested it be euthanized, I always had the dog euthanized immediately. I recall one case in particular. It was a dog attack on a person that received considerable media attention due to the severity of the wounds inflicted on the victim. I remember this tan-colored pit bull was brought into the shelter by an officer, directly after the unprovoked attack. The dog was covered in its victim's blood. His once-tan chest and shoulders were streaked with dried brown gore. Thankfully, the owner signed the dog over to Animal Control for euthanasia, but we hesitated to euthanize the animal immediately because of delayed response from the city attorney due to the media attention.

I learned my lesson quickly. That day, I received several phone calls from animal zealots who begged me not to euthanize the dog. They told me that it was not the dog's fault it had maimed the person, but the owner who was to blame. I explained to them that I probably couldn't agree with them more. However, the dog was a tower of strength and muscle, he was trained to be aggressive, and he had the experience of the attack in his mind. It was too late for him. We could not risk releasing him back into society given the possibility that he might attack or even kill another person.

Unbelievable to me, one of the women I spoke with on the phone began to call me "killer" and other more derogatory names. She told me that it was most important to keep the dog alive, regardless of the alleged risk of any further attacks on people. She showed absolutely no remorse concerning the young victim, or her family members who had just experienced this traumatic and permanently damaging incident.

I love animals. Maybe more importantly, I have a healthy respect for animals. I have seen first hand the devastation a vicious dog can inflict on a person. I keep a level head when it comes to making a decision on the life or death of a vicious animal versus the safety of human beings.

Eventually, this particular dog was euthanized, and a neighborhood filled with small children and elderly people could rest a bit more easily. Unfortunately, the young victim did not fair so well. She will always have scars (physically and mentally) that will haunt her and terrorize her.

Animal Control agencies provide many services to the communities in which they reside. They are compassionate in their rescue capacity as they save stray animals from the streets. They provide humane care for every animal with tremendous knowledge of various species from dogs and cats to wildlife. They work tirelessly to reunite pets with their owners and adopt out precious animals from the shelter. They also serve as animal law enforcement, protecting the community from dangerous animals, enforcing animal-related laws, and investigating animal abuse/cruelty cases. Animal Control is expected to perform each of these tasks and so much more on a daily basis with professionalism and dignity. It is not always easy to see an animal that is suffering or ensure safety within every neighborhood. To those of you that work in this field, volunteer at a shelter, support your local agency through rescue work, or adopt from a shelter, I personally thank and respect you for your mindfulness and dedication.

Chapter Five:
West Los Angeles Shelter, L.A., California

A Relief From the War...

As I learned about the diverse areas of Los Angeles, it seemed at first that there was no relief from the problems of pet overpopulation, euthanizing animals, animal abuse, and animal cruelty. But then there was the West Los Angeles shelter. This was a place where all of the societal rules involving animals in the city seemed not to apply. How could it be that this shelter consistently had over an eighty percent adoption rate, while the other five shelters hovered at around thirty-five percent adoptions? Chalk it up to money, money, and more money. The folks in West Los Angeles had it—and lot's of it.

The shelter itself was small, poorly designed, and very old. However, it still had a quaint feel about it and didn't seem as forbidding as some of the other city operated shelters. There were about thirty dog kennels for public viewing, with around six additional isolation kennels in the back. The cat room was small and poorly ventilated. Banks of cages numbered around twenty.

This was the only place where I can honestly say that the physical appearance of the stray dogs and cats differed from other strays in the remaining shelters. There certainly was a higher number of purebreds like the Shih Tzu that Kyra Sedgwick adopted off the Pet of the Week program. He came from the West Los Angeles shelter. Likewise, a large number of the dog owners from this area were responsible and would come to the shelter looking for and usually finding their lost pets. This was quite a change from what staff was used to experiencing at the other shelters. Because of this difference in responsible pet ownership and behavior, instead of euthanizing eighty dogs per day, the average number of animal deaths at the West Los Angeles shelter was around eight to ten dogs daily.

In exchange for all of this, the public from this area expected service, service, service. They were extremely demanding of the staff, especially the clerical employees. These residents were not used to standing in line and waiting their turn to be assisted by staff. But they also were very appreciative of staff that genuinely showed compassion for the animals under their care.

One such employee was Oscar. He was a licensed RVT and a foreign veterinarian from the Philippines. The best way to describe Oscar was by his signature smile and truly warm and cheery personality. When he first began with animal control over a decade earlier, I was told he'd had a reasonable head of hair. I only knew Oscar as an attractive, bald headed man. I am a fan of men with short hair rather than long, and shaved heads also fit into the category of a "clean cut" appearance. Anyway, it was very popular to have a shaved head, and Oscar fit right in with the trend. Everyone loved working with him. I don't think he ever had an enemy. Everyone considered him to be their friend. On top of that, he was a highly efficient and well-qualified RVT.

He fit right in with the West Los Angeles crowd. He was extremely competent in his work and was a public relations expert with the temperamental folks of this community. He was a mainstay at the West Los Angeles shelter, and I relied on him heavily in his evaluations of the animals. I valued his level head and his honesty. Oscar would check in with me when necessary, but due to his high level of competency, there were very few problems and no mistakes whenever he was on duty. When I came into the shelter to review cases and check on animals, Oscar would provide for me a medical run down of each animal. When he was finished, he would always conclude with, "Well, that's all about it." It became a term that I grew quite fond of and used often with Oscar, and in an interrelated way, I also used it when speaking with my husband. It became known as a warm and friendly way to end a conversation or discussion on a tough topic.

He was strikingly conscientious about each animal that entered the West Los Angeles shelter. He also had a sort of sixth sense about which animals had owners and which of those owners would actually come looking for their lost pets. I witnessed this special skill in Oscar myself.

During one of my regular rounds at the West Los Angeles shelter, Oscar and I were in the medical room, moving from cage to cage, examining animals with the most critical medical conditions. We regularly discussed the treatments the animals were receiving, their response to those treatments, and unfortunately, the length of time they had been in the shelter and whether or not we needed the cage space for the next animal that required advanced medical care. As we moved half way down the bank of stainless steel cages, I glanced down to the bottom row. A young, mixed breed dog met our eyes, and instantly, his tail began to flop against the cage floor, creating a tinny echo throughout the room despite the newspapers that lined the bottom of the cage. The dog did not rise. I knelt down to take a closer look and saw that Oscar had placed a Robert Jones bandage (a heavily padded bandage to immobilize a fracture prior to surgical repair) on the dog's rear limb.

"Ah, he came in a couple of days ago. Hit by car... I palpated a fracture in the rear leg, so I stabilized it. He probably also has head trauma, but the swelling around his left eye has gone down lot from yesterday," Oscar responded.

"You did a great job on the bandage," I told him.

Oscar was consistently thorough with his work. The bandage was recently applied, clean, and dry. He had also written in ink on the bandage the date of the day it was placed. This was very helpful to all the technicians, to confirm when the bandage needed changing in concert with the written orders for medical care on each animal.

"He is not eating well, so I have been hand feeding him," he added.

I carefully unhooked the stainless steel latch of the cage door, and since it was a large sized bottom level cage, I slid in and sat directly next to this sweet young dog. The dog raised his head for me, and I placed it in the palm of my left hand and gently stroked the top of his head with my right hand. Instantaneously, his eyes closed in complete contentment. I raised his upper lip to take a look at his teeth in order to make a rough estimate of his age. "He looks like he's about six months old."

"Yeah, that's what I put on the card. He is very young and sweet too, eh?" Oscar replied.

"It is so difficult watching these cases that require advanced surgical intervention, especially orthopedics, and only be able to stabilize these poor guys." I spoke my thoughts out loud...

It always was troublesome in a governmental shelter environment, knowing that a medical case could not be completely worked up due to limitations of money, equipment, and time. Many of the older shelters only had a medical room. There was no surgical suite, nothing that would fulfill sterility requirements to perform surgeries like fracture repair. We did work with off-site private veterinarians who performed advanced medical and surgical services for the shelter at reduced fees. Realistically though, they could not provide this level of service for every single stray, unowned animal that required it. They, too, were "in business" and had to charge fees for their services in order to "stay in business."

Oscar and I had just come from the main kennels where we had identified two more dogs that had come down with kennel cough, an illness contagious to all of the other dogs in the holding area. Then we were told that an animal control officer was on his way back to the shelter with a severely injured animal. That meant that we had to find cage space in the already filled medical room for three more animals. This was the worst part of the job. So many times, my staff and I stalled in making this decision in hopes that an owner would come in, just at that moment, take one of these critters home, and free up a cage. Just one cage would be helpful... Regrettably, this never happened at an opportune moment.

I reviewed the cage card in order to determine how long this young dog had been at the shelter. Unfortunately, I already knew his fate. He had been held the legal minimum holding period. He was now city property, and we could decide to hold him further for adoption or euthanize him. If his owner did not come in, we would have to try to adopt this dog out to someone who would be able to pay for close to a thousand dollars worth of surgery. That doesn't take into account the physical rehabilitation the dog would need after surgery and the emotional stress it would place on the new owner and family. Was it fair to choose a different dog for euthanasia and keep him, knowing his adoption chances would be low due to these extraneous circumstances? This is the reality of working in overcrowded governmentally operated shelters. This type of decision happens repeatedly day in and day out. There was only one certainty, and that was that a decision did indeed have to be made.

From my seated position on the bottom cage, I looked up at Oscar, waiting for him to give me an answer as to who would have to be euthanized in order to make cage space for those that legally still had additional holding time.

"Not that one," he protested as he pointed at the dog that seemed to be resting comfortably by my side. "Doc, I feel it about this one. The owner will come in. He has on an expensive collar, but without a tag. He may have lost it or something like that when he got hit."

As I looked into Oscar's deep brown eyes and listened to the desperation in his voice, I said, "You are always right about these things. I agree with you. Let's hold on to him for a while longer."

Just at that moment, I looked down at the gentle face that was still cupped in my hand, and I slowly lowered his head down to the cage floor so he could continue to rest and wait for his family to find him.

I wasn't as close to this dog as Oscar was, but I knew I had to leave the room and focus on something else or the tears would come. I quickly stood up, secured the cage, and headed for the main kennel. Oscar knew his job, knew the animals under his care. He would, and always did, make the best possible decision in such a desperate situation. Before I left the room, I turned to Oscar. "Anything else?"

He looked at me, then back to the dog with the fracture. "No, that's all about it."

Finding Nicky

I turned, followed the corridor to its end, and pulled open the heavy metal door that led to the main dog kennels. It was easy to get distracted in here, with so many dogs barking and tails wagging. As I began to look in the cages at individual dogs, I nearly bumped into a man who was walking up and down the kennel rows, attentively searching each kennel.

He had that look in his eye of a desperate pet owner who was searching for a lost pet. I stood back and watched this man for a few brief seconds, but then I became distracted. As he walked by kennel number eight, a small terrier mixed breed that appeared to have been groomed recently (actually shaved... It must have been very matted...) jumped about two and a half feet in the air to try to get the man's attention. I thought to myself, wow, that little guy really knows how to make himself be seen in order to get adopted. But the man moved on and continued to walk down the entire row of kennels. He came to the last kennel and shifted direction, sliding slowly back through the same row of kennels, just in case he missed something. He passed by kennel number ten, kennel number nine, and kennel number eight. There was that little terrier again, practicing for the Olympic jumping contest. The man ignored the dog and moved through the remaining kennels until he reached kennel number one. I looked back at kennel number eight and this dog was going crazy. He was totally out of control, barking and jumping at the kennel gate. This was more than attention-getting behavior. I was in my uniform, so I approached the gentleman.

"Excuse me, sir, can I help you?" I asked.

"Yes, I have lost my dog and was hoping someone had picked him up and brought him to the shelter. But I don't see him here," he said in a dejected tone.

"What does your dog look like?"

"Oh, he's a long-haired terrier."

My heart skipped a beat. "Are you sure this isn't your dog in kennel number eight?"

The man walked over to the front of the kennel, and the dog went ballistic and began to jump up and down more vociferously than ever.

"No, that's not my dog. He has long hair," he said disappointedly.

Quickly I grabbed the cage card that provided additional information on the animal, and sure enough there it was. "The card says that one of our volunteer groomers bathed and groomed this dog yesterday. Sir, this dog is trying to tell you something. I think this is your dog."

The man bent down to the level of the dog and said, "Nicky?" The dog would have done a double axle if he was on ice skates. He began to bark and jump at the kennel door. "Nicky, it is you!" He looked at me and said, "He turned up missing three days ago."

I scanned the card and sure enough... "He was picked up exactly three days ago," I told him.

"Well, I'll be. You little devil, I didn't even recognize you!"

I sent the man to the front clerical area to fill out the paperwork and pay the fees so he could take his dog home and free up a kennel space. After he left the kennel area, I turned to look at the shaved white terrier. I thought I heard him say, "Jesus, I'm jumping up and down, waving my paws, and crying out, Dad—yo Dad, I'm right here!"

I learned my lesson. Next time we wanted to shave down an animal, we took a "before" picture and posted it on the cage door so everyone could see exactly what the animal looked like when it came into the shelter. It is amazing how many people don't recognize their own pet with just a simple change like a haircut!

Sully and the "Orangies"

Most of my visits and observations of the animals at West L.A. began in the cat room. It was an elongated room that was split symmetrically by two doorways. One of the doors led the public from the shelter front reception to the cat viewing area. You needed to walk through the cattery to get to the dog kennels. The second door led directly into the dog kennels. As you entered, the left area of the cattery served as housing for the main population. The right side of the room contained two small banks of cages used for special condition, non-ill cats: nursing moms, older cats—anyone who required special care or who might have a compromised immune system and be more susceptible to becoming ill through close exposure to the other cats in the main population.

Also on the right side of the room was a desk that was co-occupied by the ACT working the cat room and the volunteers. There was a phone at the desk, plus brochures about spaying and neutering. Due to the traffic of staff and the public using the room as a thoroughfare, and the noise of dogs barking that resonated throughout the room each time the door to the kennels was opened, it was impossible ever to have a true conversation using that phone.

This shelter was so small that the cat room served a dual purpose and also housed rabbits. Their cages were scattered against the back wall on the left side of the room. Because of them, the room usually smelled of straw rather than cat litter, and unfortunately, some days, the room smelled strongly of urine from an adult male, unneutered rabbit. These big males obviously had no manners because they preferred to "spray" rather than use their litter box. This was probably a good indicator as to why their owners turned them in to the shelter.

One of the ACTs had decorated the walls of the room with a variety of colorful photographs of cats from magazines, newsletters, and calendars. That really cheered up the place, and I noticed the public spent time looking at these pictures, picking out what looked like the pet they had at home or the pet they hoped to find at the shelter that day.

My routine was to methodically walk from cage to cage, checking out all three levels, to see the number, type, and condition of the cats in the main housing area. My weakness was any orange tabby cat, especially those with orange eyes. Every veterinarian knows that the most sociable cat (scientifically proven, of course) is the male orange tabby with orange eyes. As I explained in the introduction to this book, Benjamin, the resident cat at the veterinary hospital where I worked for most of my high school and college days, was an orange tabby. I also had one named Tom while I was in veterinary school. He was such a nut! He even learned how to balance three ball point pens on his head at once. He knew I needed entertainment during study breaks so he happily obliged.

To give you an example of his social skills, I used to throw birthday parties in Tom's honor. (Yes, veterinary school can sometimes make you crazy.) He would respectfully receive the party guests by seating himself on a stool positioned close to the front door. As each guest entered the party, he would tip his head to them, and in return, would receive a pat on the head or birthday salutations. When everyone had arrived, Tom knew it was time to mingle. He promptly left his position on the stool and moved through the crowd, rubbing against people's legs and occasionally jumping confidently into a lonely lap. Anyway, that's where my adoration for orange tabbies originated.

As I continued my walk through, of course I was keeping my eye out for any orange tabbies. If I found one, I usually had to open that cage, pull the big guy out, and either hold him draped over my shoulder or give him the real test, which was to cuddle him upside down close to my chest. He passed the test if instantaneous purring resulted—and I can say that I was rarely disappointed. Many staff members knew of my soft spot for these "orangies," and the West L.A. Senior ACT, Sully, was no exception. One day, I must have been entranced with my observations because I did not even hear Sully enter the cattery. I looked up when I heard a loud, commanding voice say, "All orange tabbies scheduled for euthanasia today."

As soon as I saw Sully, I knew it was a trick, and I immediately put on the biggest pout I could muster. Simultaneously, I raised my eyebrows, crinkling my brow with such force that anyone watching would have been sure that tears were to follow. But when his eyes met mine, they softened, and he sheepishly scrunched his neck down below his shoulders and said, "Hey Doc, you know I was only kidd'n."

Sully was always giving me a hard time—but in a good way. If I'd seen him moving down the corridor to the cat room where I encountered him that day, I would have described his gait as a confident swagger, reminiscent of the famous walk by Richard Gere in the beginning of the movie, "American Gigolo." Sully was a foreign veterinarian like Oscar, but he had graduated from professional school in Mexico. He chose to stay away from the medical work in the sheltering environment and preferred the kennel management aspect of the job. He was slender and tall, and the manner in which he carried himself clearly delivered the subliminal message that he knew he was quite good looking.

I noticed that he was never questioned why he didn't wear the standard white t-shirt under the uniform. His uniform shirt was worn "commando" style and always unbuttoned one extra button in order to expose a patch of chest hairs that just couldn't seem to stay hidden and came bellowing over the uniform seam. His Mexican accent was profound and became thicker when necessary as situations called for it. His humor and mannerisms were fortunately irrepressible. I could spend hours just listening to him explain a situation or describe an experience that he had been involved with earlier. He was a remarkable breath of fresh air in the world of sheltering, which often times can be depressing and sinister. Many of my fondest memories of my shelter work in Los Angeles are of the comical and profoundly individual encounters I shared with Sully.

When I told him what had just happened with the small white terrier, Nicky, he flashed me a crooked smile using only the right side of his upper and lower lip, and with a soothing Spanish accent he said, "Hey Doc, you should coome here more often. Good things happen here at the Vest L.A. shellter."

Just at that moment, I came upon an orange tabby. Of course, all of the cage doors were locked. I quickly turned to Sully, and before I could ask him to unlock it for me, he reached for the massive key chain that was hooked to his belt. He rolled his eyes, grasped the lock, turned the key, and opened the cage door. He gently grabbed the big orange Tom cat and handed him to me. "You know, Doc, you are just a big softie."

I chose not to listen to him at that point because all I could hear was a deep rumble in my ear from the purring, and all I could feel was the tickling of long cat whiskers. My therapy for the day had been completed. After a few minutes, I replaced the cat back in the cage and secured the lock.

Love the "Orangies" — my kitty Bartie.

Sully and the Dog Thief

I asked Sully how it had been going. He said, "Just a regular day... O.J. was here to pick up his dog... 'ya know."

"What?"

"Yeah, we all posed for a picture with him. It's on my desk. Come, I will show it to you."

I followed Sully out of the cat room and into the clerical area where his desk was located in a small cubicle. Sure enough, there it was. Among pictures of his kids, fellow workers, and his airplane was a picture of the infamous O.J. Simpson flanked by Sully, the West L.A. kennel staff, and officers.

"What's the story behind this?" I asked.

"He's got a big black Dane that keeps getting out. This is about the second time we picked up the dog and brought him in. O.J. comes right away to pick him up and pay the fees."

"Is the dog neutered?"

Sully just looked at me and gave me the usual, "'Ya know these guys...'"

Sully was now seated at his desk, and I could tell that he was about to share another story with me. He made himself more comfortable and leaned back in the desk chair. I sat on the edge of his desk and settled in for the long haul.

"You should have been here yesterday, Doc. Oh my God, what a crazy one we had."

"What do you mean?" I asked cautiously.

"This guy brings this small black dog into the shelter a few days ago because he found the dog on the street and he was busted up a little. So we put the dog in the back in the medical room. The guy comes every day to visit the dog and starts crying and shit. He keeps telling me that he knows I'm going to kill the dog. I tell him every day, 'Look Man, I'm not killing the dog. When the dog comes available for adoption, you can pay for him and take him home.' He came today to adopt the dog, but yesterday, the guy was crazy—you know what I mean?"

I learned long ago that I should just nod until Sully finished telling his story. Sully received the customary nod from me and continued.

"So yesterday, he was in the back in the medical area looking at the dog, and all of a sudden, the fucker grabs the dog and starts running out of the room. I am standing there with him, and he steals the dog right in front of me. But the guy is so stupid, you know? Instead of running for the exit, he runs the other way towards the dog kennels. So I run from the outside and bolt the perimeter doors to the kennels and trap him inside. I know I got him now, so I just sit back and wait. I am looking through the small window on the door leading to the kennel corridor, just watching the guy, who knows that he's caught. You aren't going to believe this, but just about this time, I turn around and see the Director of the Department coming down the hallway—'ya know, Mr. Big Wig. He comes up to me all smiles, says, 'Hi, Sully,' and introduces whoever is with him. Then he says he wants a tour of the kennels. I have my foot against the bolted door leading to the kennels, and I say, 'It isn't really a good time.' But you know these important guys... He insists. I have to be a little bit stronger, but I am still trying to be nice to him and say, 'Hey Man, this really isn't a good time.' He must have understood, and he said he would return later."

About this time, I have to start cracking up with laughter. This whole situation is so bizarre, yet commonplace in one of the shelters.

Sully continues, "I look back through the window, and the guy who tried to steal the dog is looking back at me with this dog in his arms. He falls to his knees and starts crying. I open the door and just look at him. Pretty soon I'm looking at the guy and say, 'What the hell is wrong with you, man?' The guy looks at me, and in between sobs says, 'I just couldn't stand him being here any longer.'"

"How did you end up?" I asked.

"He gave me the dog back and returned today to adopt it. Doc, what's the matter with these people? They crazy."

"Did you ever let the Director know what was going down?"

"No. I guess I should do that," he conceded.

I shook my head and thought to myself that this was just another example of how emotionally involved people who came to the shelter could become with the animals we cared for. This man had been willing to go to jail for stealing this dog when, in less than twenty-four hours, he could come in and adopt it.

Crazy About Animals

I recall speaking with an extreme animal rights person who tried to explain to me her feelings for animals. She used a pictorial example to help me understand. She said if we were at the ocean on a beach and a person was drowning and at the same time a cat was drowning, she would save the cat and forgo saving the person. I sat back for a minute and finally understood why it continued to be next to impossible to communicate and reason with some of these folks. Not only would we never be on the same page, but justifiable dialogue seemed to be out of reach. Nevertheless, the politicians, who received outlandish and fabricated complaints about the operations of animal control from zealots among the animal rights crowd, told us we had to, not only work with them, but give them whatever they were asking for, so that they would stop taking up the politicians' time with complaints. Basically, the politicians just wanted the problem to go away at whatever cost.

Usually, that cost was on the animals' and employees' sides. This is one aspect of animal control that was frustrating, exhausting, and counterproductive. The extra time we should have been spending with the animals often went to lengthy meetings and extraneous conversations, conversations that continually circled back to the underlying philosophy exhibited by the "saving the drowning cat" example. You could drive yourself crazy trying to please everyone and especially these people. Survival and sanity at animal control depended on confidence in yourself as a humanitarian for both animals and people. If you could feel with your heart and then use your head to check yourself and make the final decision, you usually stayed on track.

The political aspect of the job never ceased to amaze me. Not only did the politicians try to divert animal extremists from their offices so they didn't have to continually hear their complaints, but they also became creative in ways to silence them by dealing out special favors. I can recall one of these favors in particular—appointing an individual to our Commission Board per the request of an extremist. The appointee made policy suggestions and requests of the shelters as directed by the extremist. We all knew what was going down, but until this individual was removed from the Commission, we were obliged to look into his obscure requests. But we all did so cautiously because we knew his objective was to gather information and report back to the extremist.

This appointee seemed always to demand extra privileges and access at the West L.A. shelter. I can recall one morning receiving a phone call from Sully. "Hey Doc, I got this crazy guy here says he wants to see the euthanasia room. Says he's a commissioner... I don't have to let him in do I? He seems a little nuts."

I asked Sully to describe him to me, and sure enough, it was the new commissioner. I told Sully to put him on the phone and I would talk to him.

I could hear Sully in the background, "Hey man, the Doc wants to talk to you."

Within a few minutes on the phone with him, I understood that reasoning with him was not going to be an option. The euthanasia room was for employees only and for good reason. All of the employees were trained for safety in this area. Often there were dangerous animals, and dangerous situations could arise in this room. But most importantly, I didn't know how emotionally stable this guy was, and I didn't know if he could handle the stress of the situation, so I denied him access to the euthanasia room. He was furious. He told me I had to do whatever he said. I told him I respectfully disagreed and he was not gaining access to that room until I was comfortable that he had received the proper training. I knew this wouldn't go over well, but it did actually work.

Sully got back on the line and said, "I don't know what you said to him, but he is really pissed off and just left the shelter."

I don't know what the Commissioner was looking for or was expecting to find, but my biggest concern was that I couldn't be sure he wouldn't fabricate some story about what he saw in the room or didn't see. It just wasn't worth the risk to me.

I knew Sully could handle him if he came by again, so I wasn't worried. I always watched out for my crew and tried to divert the trouble makers from them. They had enough stress to worry about with the daily operations at the shelter.

With a slight grin Sully said, "Way to have our backs, Doc. Hey, next time you come out here, Oscar and I will take you to this new restaurant for lunch—really nice... I think you will like it. And of course, you will be with two good-looking guys, sooo how about it?"

I had to laugh to myself. Of course I would save a lunch date for two of my favorite guys. I just wish they had a little more confidence—Ha!

Chapter Six:
Harbor Shelter, San Pedro, California

Taking Gus to the Scene of the Crime

The shelter in the most southern district of Los Angeles was located in San Pedro. It was called the Harbor shelter for its proximity to the Los Angeles international harbor. The big city of Long Beach bordered one side of San Pedro while Terminal Island, an industrial small island, was located on another side. The rough city of Wilmington also bordered this seaside town. Two major freeways ended (or started, depending on your orientation) at this major hub. They are the 710 freeway, which is well known for its semi-truck traffic to and from the containers that are delivered to the harbor, and the 110 freeway. The city of San Pedro had a wide range of inhabitants. It was basically an old fishing town with nice homes, especially as you moved toward the town of Palos Verdes, as well as homes in a low socioeconomic state with American veterans, families of diverse ethnicity, and an elderly population all trying to reside together. The neighboring city of Wilmington was well known for its poverty-level inhabitants, drug dealers, gang members, and as I came to find out, dog fighters.

I remember it was about 6:30 in the morning, and I was just thinking about getting out of bed and getting ready for work at my home in Long Beach. My husband and I continued with our long distance relationship, and I saw him on weekends when he flew down from Sacramento. It was helpful that he was also a veterinarian and that he understood most of the issues that came up with animal control. But unfortunately, communication during the week had to be by telephone late in the evenings, and especially early in the morning like this, it seemed very lonely.

I shifted my Boston Terrier and my Greyhound over a few feet in bed in order to throw my legs over the side of the mattress and allow my feet to reach the Berber carpet on the bedroom floor. My dogs were wonderful companions, especially my Boston who had been my best friend since I was a sophomore in veterinary school, but they never could entirely compensate for the days I was without my husband. It was a welcome respite when family members or friends would come by and stay with me on occasion. The previous night, my brother Gus came over. He was a professional photographer, and he had come up to Long Beach to get some shots of the beach and the ocean. By the time he was finished with his work (you know photographers... they will wait for hours for just the precise lighting...) it was too late for him to make the drive to his home in San Diego, so we ate dinner, we had some catch up time, and he spent the night.

I was moving toward the bathroom sink to do the morning face washing ritual when the phone rang. Now a phone call that early in the morning meant one of two things. Either someone in your immediate family had an emergency or there was some traumatic event that happened at work. I ran for the phone and caught it on the second ring, hoping it didn't wake my brother up.

"Hello," I answered anxiously.

The voice on the other end was easily recognizable as the nervous, yet-to-be-permanently-appointed Lieutenant from the Harbor shelter. "Doc, we got a real disaster out here. How fast can you get here?"

"Lieutenant Dulce, where are you?"

"I'm on my way to Wilmington, to the scene of the investigation of a case that the graveyard shift ACO has been working on since about 3:00 A.M. She is telling me that there was some dog fight out there, and both dogs are dead. One was burned alive."

"Oh my God! Anyone in custody?"

"Not yet, but I think there are some witnesses. We are going to need you to examine the dogs, gather evidence, talk to potential witnesses... You know the drill."

"Is everything still just as the officer found it, or have the animals been moved?" I asked with a bit of hope in my voice.

"The cops are out there with her, and they ain't moved a thing. They are waiting for us to come out since it's our investigation."

"Any press on site?"

"Press?" he comically responded. "Come on Doc, it's Wilmington. They probably had a couple robberies and a murder last night. This ain't big news by any PD standards."

"This should be quite a case for us on animal cruelty. By lucky coincidence, my brother is staying with me, and he's a professional photographer. Think I should bring him with me to take some photos that may help us out later in court?"

"Yeah, sure, bring him along. Just hurry up and get here. You will see our trucks, and PD is with us. I told 'em we are only staying in that area as long as we have a PD unit with us."

Then the phone line went dead, and my heart began to pound. My first thought was of a dog, really any living thing, being burned alive. I got a cold chill down my spine and figured today would be another day of visualizing something I had never seen before and hoped I would never see again. It seemed like this job just kept doing that to me, and every day was a new experience. I quickly changed into my veterinary uniform and went to inform my brother of the situation.

Gus agreed to help me out that morning and accompanied me on the relatively short drive to Wilmington. "You are so lucky that I brought extra film with me and that I have all of my gear," Gus said nonchalantly as he peered through the dirty side window of my city-issued vehicle. "Don't you ever wash this thing?" he asked.

My brother was a stickler for details, including cleanliness. God knows how many times a day he showered, made sure his living space was clean, etc. And don't think I wasn't a sister in the true sense of the word. I heckled him about all of this whenever possible. He approached his photography work the same way. He meticulously cleaned the lenses of all of his cameras, had cases for each piece of equipment, and used special bags and containers for his film. He traveled quite a bit and even lived in Italy for many years (where he met his wife), so he also had special canisters that protected his film when he went through the airline security systems before boarding a plane. You always knew when Gus was visiting your home because you could open up your refrigerator in the kitchen and find an entire shelf that had been rearranged in order to hold boxes of soon-to-be-used film. The refrigeration temperature was just what the eccentric artist/photographer ordered to guarantee that each picture taken with that film would be of the maximum clarity the film would allow.

So it would be that I'd be spending an entire day with my brother in one of the scariest, most poverty-stricken areas in the Harbor's district. I kind of didn't tell him that part of the deal.

The Ocean Breeze Can't Camouflage Every Torment...

"Gus, you really have to pay attention out here," I started to lecture him. "This is a really dangerous part of town, and we already have PD on site, so don't go wandering off by yourself in order to get the perfect picture or anything."

"Pff," he hissed back at me. "PD? Is that bad boy lingo for police department?"

"Yes, it is. And you better listen to them."

"You really like this tough guy stuff don't you?" he asked with snark in his tone.

"Actually, I do like the law enforcement part of the job." What I didn't tell him was that it was one of the best parts of the job. Animal abuse and cruelty appalled me, but instead of just getting upset over it, by working with animal control, I (we) had the authority to do something about it. Through my years with animal control, I had worked with city attorneys on cases, testified in court, and even become an expert witness against the so-called "sport" of dog fighting. I guess I should have gotten into law enforcement, but with my five-foot five lean frame, it would have always been a physical challenge. As my thoughts drifted, Gus continued.

"Don't you think I have been in places like this before? I did go to school right smack in the middle of the worst part of Chicago. I have had my share of people chasing me. Try running with all of this equipment over your back."

I had to laugh and said, "Why would anyone be chasing you?"

"I guess it had something to do with the fact that I had my camera set up on the tripod, and I was taking a shot of the sunset. Unfortunately, this guy thought I was photographing what he was doing in his backyard."

"Well, were you?"

"I wasn't exactly photographing it, but you could say I was looking a little bit. I couldn't help it. I could see directly over his fence."

"What was he doing?"

"It wasn't just him, but the woman with him. I don't think she appreciated having me that close to their fence either." He gave the characteristic infantile laugh that I had grown up with and known all my life. It hadn't changed in all of those years, and it still sounded the same way it did when he used to get excited over something Captain Kirk did during a Star Trek episode.

"For God's sake," I said. "You probably deserved to get caught."

"Perhaps," he sighed with a bit of arrogance. "But you have never seen anyone pack up a tripod faster, not to mention hoisting twenty-five pounds of camera gear into their backpack. I was hauling, baby. I guess I had no choice with this ex-high school looking football player after me."

Gus was never a fan of "jocks," and I guess his lack of admiration for this type continued even post-graduate school. I just shook my head and wondered as I always did why he hadn't had the crap beaten out of him yet. He is just one of those lucky guys, always in the wrong place at the wrong time and just getting away with it by the skin of his teeth.

Just as we were finishing that stimulating discussion, I turned the corner and saw three animal control collection vehicles and two PD units. I parked the car on the street and told Gus to leave his equipment in the car. We would lock it, and since the car would be in our view, there shouldn't be a problem.

"Are you crazy? This equipment sticks with me like an appendage. Hey, that's veterinarian talk, huh? I am certainly not leaving anything in this car, in this neighborhood," he told me emphatically.

We met up with the investigators and got the low down on the incident that had occurred late the night before. The graveyard Animal Control Officer (ACO) told the story as she knew it. She was shorter than I was and probably stood five feet, one inch, tall, but she was a lot stockier than I was. I thought it was extremely dangerous to have anyone, man or woman, on the midnight to 8:00 A.M. shift driving around the streets on patrol alone in South Los Angeles and this Wilmington area. But all of the female ACOs told me that they took turns with these shifts and locations just like the guys. It was another thing they had to do to be accepted in to the good 'ol boys' club. Women had only been allowed to be ACOs for about 12-15 years, and in the beginning, they were sparse indeed.

The ACO we were working with this morning looked tired, and as I looked at my watch, I knew that she was already into about the second hour of her overtime for today. I had this feeling that it was going to be a lot longer before we were through.

"I received a call from dispatch around 3:00 A.M. to respond to a complaint about an injured dog," she began. "When I got on the scene, one of the neighbors led me into that alley over there." She pointed about one hundred feet down the road to the entrance of an alley that had backyards bordering each side of it. "That's where I found the first dog. It is pretty deesgusting. It's a big pit that someone chained to a telephone pole, and the guy is burned all over his body. He's dead, and I left him there so you could see him and we could get pictures." She took a deep breath and continued. "About a block away, I found another dog laying on his side, next to the curb on the street with gun shot wounds to the chest. There's a trail of blood over there like he walked a bit after being shot, but he's dead too."

"Also a pit?" I asked.

"Yes. The neighbors have been telling me about a dog fight that happened around here last night. The big macho dog of the neighborhood lost the match. I guess they were kind of pissed off, so they decided to kill the winner. That's the dog that they burned alive. Then I guess they were so humiliated by losing the fight that the owner of the loser shot his own dog. This whole thing is sickening. I interviewed a few people, and you can tell that they know who owned these dogs and who were involved with all of this. I still have a lot more people to interview, but now that it's daylight, everyone in this neighborhood is getting afraid to talk to us. In that dumpster by the alley where the burned dog is, I saw some rags that smelled like they had accelerant on them. I need to go back over there and gather that evidence and question the people in the house that live near there."

"OK," I said. "This is my brother, Gus. He is going to be our evidence photographer for the day. Can we make sure that no one touches these dogs until we get the pictures and gather any evidence in the area?"

"Yes, PD has both streets secured, and an officer is on the other street with the dog that was shot so nobody messes with it," she replied.

"Alright, I would like to start with the burned dog first. Gus and I will go down the alley and check it out."

Gus and I walked about half way down the back alley, and we would have known we were getting close to the body of the dog even if our eyes had been closed. Our noses became acutely aware of burned flesh. I can describe it like a kitchen that is filled with toasters, all of them with slices of burning bread in them. You know how that smell lingers throughout your house if you just burn one slice? Well, out in the open, supposedly in fresh air, you could still smell it—a personification of hundreds of slices of burned toast. It not only had a rotten smell to it, it also had the sickly-sweet smell of pus oozing from areas of skin that were not totally charred. Even today, when Gus and I talk about that day in the alley, we both agree. We can close our eyes and still smell that burned dog. We can be right back in that alley in those revolting circumstances.

The Investigation Begins in Earnest

We saw the wooden telephone pole that the dog was chained to as described by the ACO. I approached the body, and without saying a word, I pulled the plastic gloves from my back pocket and placed them on each hand. Then I knelt down and studied every detail about the situation. Those details have been forever burned into my memory.

There was no way to tell what color the dog was because its entire body was charred a deep black. He looked to weigh around sixty or seventy pounds. I looked at the dog's head, the shape of the jaw line, the ears, and the muscles of the neck, and unquestionably, this was a pit bull. He was lying on his side with all four of his limbs extended straight out, very similar to a dog displaying tetanic seizures. One end of a large linked chain was wrapped around his neck several times while the other end was wrapped around the base of the telephone pole.

The distance between the dog's head and the pole was barely a few inches. From the looks of it, the dog probably was unable to move at all from the position in which we had found him. I looked more closely at his face. His expression had been frozen (in this case, "burned" in time. His upper and lower lips were slightly parted, and his teeth were barred, validating the pain he must have endured. At this point, I didn't know if I could look any further, but at the same time, I could not take my eyes off of the agony that was displayed through this animal's expression.

Gus was looking over my shoulder, assessing how he would be taking photographs of this wretched scene. I finally looked down at the remainder of the dog's body. I reached out with my right gloved hand and placed it on the dog's chest. I just needed to have some form of contact with this poor animal. Then my eyes traced their way down his abdomen and ended at his tail. I know Gus must have been following my examination because when our eyes reached the rear of the dog, I heard him gasp. I was pretty sure I knew what he saw, even though I never asked him. Even the testicles of this creature had been burned coal black.

I stood up, removed my gloves, and replaced them in my back pocket. Gus spent the next ten minutes maneuvering around the dog, clicking away from every angle he could get. When he said he thought he had captured the incident, we decided to walk the remainder of the alley to see if there might be any other evidence from the crime. We both walked down the middle of the alley. It was bordered on either side by chain link or wooden paneled fences enclosing small backyards to impoverished homes.

As we walked by the first yard, we were startled by the charge of a large, tan pit bull. He impacted the steel chain link fence with his chest and shoulders. I could feel his hot breath against the side of my uniform pants, and I quickly moved farther toward the opposite side of the alley. His barking and growling set off the alarm for all of the other outdoor watchdogs that lived along this alley, and soon, more than ten dogs were out in full defense of their property. As we passed some of these backyards, our only protection from these massive beasts was a flimsy fence. At that point, Gus and I looked at each other. There was no way we could concentrate and look for evidence. It just wasn't a secure location. We did an about-face and hurried back down the alley to join the rest of the investigation team.

We informed the Lieutenant that we'd photographed the burned dog and that, after he had gathered any additional evidence from the area that he needed, the body could be removed and transported back to the shelter so that we could perform a full necropsy (an autopsy in human terms).

The next step was to photograph the dog on the next block, the one that had been shot. Gus and I walked over and talked to the police officer who was securing the opposite side of the alley and street.

"I see a lot of things on my beat, but this is pretty bad," remarked the officer. "These people around here have no respect for life."

Gus and I approached the dog executed by gunshot. It was half in the street and half lying against the curb. His body was soaked in a pool of blood, and as I looked up, I saw footprints of blood extending from the rear of the body to the other side of the street. "Gus, you have got to photograph these blood stains coming from across the street," I said.

"No chance... It is way too bright out here, and with the color of the cement on the street, it will never show up in a photograph," he responded.

I couldn't just let this pass, so I thought for a minute, told Gus I would be right back, and ran back to our car. I returned with a box full of Latex disposable gloves. I always carried a box with me in the car because I never knew from day to day what I would encounter, and I always tried to be prepared and safe. Gus looked at me and said, "What are you going to do with those?"

"What if we mark the trail of bloody prints with the gloves? I will place the gloves parallel to the footprints, and then you can photograph the gloves. Will they show up on a photo?"

"That's a pretty good idea. Let's see if it works."

I began tracing the steps of the dog by placing Latex gloves along the trail of blood from one side of the street to the other. I felt like I was Gretel, from Hansel and Gretel, leaving a trail of breadcrumbs in order to find my way home. When I was done tracing the path, I stepped back and took a look. It had worked. The footprints were now readily visualized, and Gus began snapping away.

After we finished with those photos, we centered our attention on the dog's body. It too was a pit bull, tan in color, a male of about seventy to seventy-five pounds. Like the first dog, he was stout and muscular. The wounds in his chest were consistent in size with a shotgun injury. There was also blood from his right shoulder area, with possible injuries at that location too.

We continued to take our photographs at the scene and were joined by the investigating ACO. She let us know that the police had just interviewed a neighbor who allegedly identified the shooter, and we were all heading over to his house a few blocks away. I let her know that the dog that was shot could be picked up and also taken back to the shelter for a necropsy. We hoped to recover the shotgun pellets, pellets that could be matched to a weapon if one was recovered.

A Wealth of Evidence

We all got into our cars and caravanned over to the house in question. When we arrived, a team of plain-clothed police investigators was already on the scene and had gained entry into the house. One of the officers at the front door told us that the house was secured and that we could enter and assist in looking for additional evidence.

"Additional evidence?" I asked the officer.

"Yeah, when we came up on the property, we found this," the officer stated portentiously. He pointed to a shotgun that was placed next to him along with other pieces of evidence that he was monitoring. "The gun was lying on top of these shrubs by the front door as we came up the front walk."

I looked up the walkway that led from the street to the front door of the house. Sure enough, there was a low hedge that bordered it and extended to the front patio. It sounded like the guy just decided to dump the weapon and threw it into the bushes outside his front door. Was he hoping no one would look for it out there? Criminals never cease to amaze me... how they seem to set themselves up constantly...

The officer continued, "Then the guy answers the front door with no shirt on and jeans that have blood stains all over the front of them. We look through the front door and see a lit reefer sitting on the table. So we bust the guy. His mother comes running out and says it's her pot, not the kid's. We find out that the kid just got out of jail and is on probation. If he violates, he goes right back in. I guess she thought if she took the blame for the pot that we would let him go." The officer shook his head and gave me a crooked smile like he had seen all of this many times before.

Gus and I entered the house. Several detectives and uniformed officers were going through the place. They were opening drawers and cabinets and searching in closets for whatever evidence they could find. This was a pretty rough neighborhood, filled with gangs and no doubt hard core drugs, which also meant the presence of used needles. I pulled my plastic gloves from my back pocket, put them on, and then placed my leather gloves over them before I started touching anything in the house. Maybe I knew too much about disease transmission, but I wasn't about to take a chance rummaging through a drawer and coming in contact with a dirty hypodermic needle.

As I looked at the detectives, I noticed that none of them were wearing gloves. They were blindly reaching into drawers and pulling items out of closets with their bare hands. "Aren't you guys worried about coming in contact with sharp objects?" I sheepishly inquired.

The older detective looked up at me and said, "I've been doing this for a long time. I guess I am immune to a lot of that kind of stuff."

I smiled and nodded my head. I didn't think this was the time or place to educate him on the transmission of diseases like hepatitis or HIV. In fact, he was not immune to any of that.

Just about at that moment, Lieutenant Dulce caught my attention and motioned for me to come outside. I told Gus to follow me. He took one more shot of the police conducting their search, and we both went to the side yard.

As I walked outside, I took greater notice of my surroundings. Each of the houses on this block was exactly the same. I believe this area was part of a housing project—a housing project that had gone bad. The small square-shaped houses were run down, but all had front patios. Across the street, I noticed that the "home boys" had gathered on the front patio of one of the houses. There were probably seven to ten of them watching every single thing we were doing and especially what the police were doing.

This particular street backed up to the freeway, and a large concrete sound barrier wall separated the neighborhood from the busy freeway. The wall was covered in graffiti. A variety of colors, symbols, and terms graced that wall. In a way, it was kind of artistic and tell-tale of the area we were visiting. Just at that moment, I happened to look over at Gus who must have been thinking the same thing because he was lifting his camera to photograph that wall. In order to position his camera for the shot, he had to sweep the camera past the house where the "home boys" were resting. It was like a movie. The minute Gus panned his camera past that house in preparation for the photo of the wall, all of the "boys" ducked beneath the railing in fear that they would be photographed.

One of the officers came over to Gus and asked him, "Are you crazy trying to photograph those guys? Most of them have criminal records, and many probably have warrants out for their arrest. Are you trying to get shot or something?"

Gus didn't even respond, but he lowered his camera and instantaneously, the faces of the "boys" began to emerge from below the railing. This time, they weren't smiling or laughing. I did hear quite a bit of street talk and rapping. I pulled Gus out of the situation and over to the side yard to meet up with Lieutenant Dulce.

Interviewing the Witness/Returning to Base

There was a non-mobile trailer deposited on a small grassy area between the two houses. (Parked would be the wrong word to describe how the vehicle was placed in the yard.) Dulce told us that we had to come over and talk to the guy who lived inside. "This guy is tripp'n," he said.

We approached the door of the trailer, and the Lieutenant knocked loudly. The door opened, and a gray-haired, worn-looking man appeared. Emerging with him were puffs of smoke, and out wafted the odor of marijuana. I looked more closely, and my eyes began to hurt in sympathy as I saw how red and irritated the eyes of this man were. Lieutenant Dulce asked the man to tell me what he had told him earlier about the dogs.

"Well, I know them dogs. Well at least I knows one of them. He found that there dog a few months ago and decided he would keep him on account of his big size and all. He chained him right out back there to that there dog house." He pointed a few feet from his trailer to a beat up dog house with chain on tether and no dog attached to it. "Them guys fight these dogs. I seen 'em do it before. You can look for youselves in the back there. That's where they do it."

"Do you see them do this during the day or at night?" I asked him.

"Well, I'm a hairdresser, so I work during the day. I don't see much then," he responded.

I hesitated for a minute because Lieutenant Dulce had his head down and was snickering a bit. I could understand why. I looked at this old man with thin, wispy, grey hair that was blowing in the wind and standing straight up in the air. A hairdresser, I thought? Sure enough... and why wasn't he working today? All good questions that I was pretty confident I already knew the answers to...

Lieutenant Dulce, Gus, and I left the old man and proceeded to walk to the back area where he told us the fights were staged. I looked at the Lieutenant and said, "Hey Lieutenant, you are in luck. It looks like you might need a trim. I'm sure your new friend in the trailer could probably take care of that for you right now." Dulce just looked at me, smiled, and nodded in agreement with my assessment of the old man.

The three of us walked around to the back of the house where a small square cement area was conveniently hidden from the street about forty feet away. As we walked onto the cement, we noted blood stains in the center. Most dog fighters create some sort of fighting ring when they set up a match, and it appeared that this cemented area served that purpose. Gus took some photos, and Lieutenant Dulce seemed quite happy that we had identified the fighting location.

By now it was early afternoon, and I still needed to get back to the Harbor shelter and perform necropsies on both dogs. Gus and I left Dulce and the other officers at the site, and we got back into my city vehicle and headed for San Pedro. We radioed ahead our estimated time of arrival, and when we pulled into the front of the shelter, Todd was waiting for us and unlocked the drive-through gate.

Todd was the lead Registered Veterinary Technician (RVT) at Harbor. I don't ever remember a time when he wasn't congenial and polite. His distinctive smile automatically drew your eyes to his round face and brown button eyes. He too was of Philippine origin and was a foreign veterinarian like Oscar from the West Los Angeles shelter. He was a few inches taller than I was and of stocky build. He was very capable of animal medical care and moved with confidence when handling and examining animals. He never balked at any task I asked him to do at the shelter, and he always answered with a reassuring, "Doc don't worry, no problem."

Gus and I pulled through the gate, and I rolled down my window to greet Todd. "Hey," I said in an exasperated tone, "did you hear about our investigation?"

"Oh my God, Doc, it is awful. The dogs are back in the medical room waiting for you. I have everything all set up," he responded.

Gus and I parked the car in a very small cemented area confined within the shelter property. It served many purposes. It was a public walkway to and from the dog and cat areas. It was used as a parking lot for employees and patrol vehicles. And a section was devoted to a wash rack for the vehicles and an animal loading and unloading area for the officers.

We pulled ourselves out of the car, walked to the far end of the shelter property, and entered into the tiny medical room where Todd was waiting for us. The room was so small, and the stainless steel examination table in the center of the room took up so much space, that it was hard to maneuver around it in order to get to the sink at the opposite side of the room and wash your hands. A small desk and filing cabinet were positioned to the left of the entrance to the room. Todd kept his logs there, all organized on separate clipboards. There were medical treatment logs, pharmaceutical logs, animal inventory logs, and the dreaded euthanasia log.

Directly above the desk on the wall, Todd had a photograph of himself in surgical scrubs leaning against an anesthesia machine. This photo was taken while Todd was working in the research industry as a technician at the local university. I was always amazed how quickly Todd had caught on to the rules and protocols of animal control, considering he had no background at all in this animal specialty. It is very complicated, with legal holding periods for animals, special rules for evidence animals, dangerous animals that are awaiting a hearing, animals that are quarantined for rabies... The list of special categories goes on and on.

Todd was one of the last Philippino recruits to join our animal care team, and at first, he was the most difficult for me to understand because he had a strong accent, and when he was nervous, he accompanied some of his speech passages with a slight giggle. Now that we had been working together for over a year and he knew I had complete confidence in his abilities and his dependability at the shelter, the initial communication gap had disappeared.

The burned dog was in the center of the room. Todd had respectfully placed towels on the cold examination table and then placed the body of the dog on top of them. That look of torment remained on the dog's face, and I grabbed another towel and softly placed it over his head and neck. "OK," I said, "let's get started."

The Necropsies

Gus photographed as Todd and I carefully examined the body. We converted our visual observations into a written report as we proceeded. Due to the condition of the skin from the burning, it was impossible to identify other injuries like puncture (bite) wounds that may have occurred during the dogfight. The remainder of the external examination indicated that one hundred percent of the body had third degree burns. The conclusions from our internal examination indicated changes in the lungs and chest consistent with death caused by severe burn injuries.

The size of the room didn't allow for much ventilation, and within ten minutes, the charred smell was overwhelming and seemed carcinogenic. Todd carefully placed the dog's body in a plastic bag when the examination was completed and carried it to the refrigeration area to await the daily dead animal pick up. We left the door to the room ajar as we waited for Todd to come back.

When he returned to the medical room, he carried the body of the second dog, the one that was shot. Now, upon closer examination, we could really see the damage to the chest that the gunshot had caused. We identified two separate entry sites, one in the chest and the other in the shoulder. This dog also had puncture wounds in the neck as well as tears in the left ear. I carefully debrided away skin from around the chest gunshot wound and located buckshot that had lodged in various muscle bellies throughout the chest area. I collected a sampling of the small pellets and placed them in a specimen jar so that we could match these pellets with the ammunition that was found at the suspect's house. I did the same for the pellets that were embedded into the shoulder muscles. The shot to the chest had caused severe damage to the heart and was the cause of death.

Todd removed this body too while I completed the written report. I looked over at Gus, and he was now sitting in one of the small institutional chairs against the wall, looking rather spent.

He looked at me and said, "I will never forget this day, nor will I forget this smell."

I gave him a weary nod, and my thoughts drifted back to the torture and anguish both dogs had experienced over the last twenty-four hours, first through being forced to engage in an organized dogfight, then through each of their individual, revolting deaths. If we were to fast-forward in time with this particular case, the results would be as follows. We were able to match the shotgun pellets with the firearm found at the suspect's house. However, the dog-fighting charges against the suspect who owned the gun were used as bargaining chips for charges holding higher criminal penalties. That is, the lesser charge of dog fighting was dropped in lieu of the charges of possession of a firearm and drugs. Ultimately, this led to a felony conviction, and the bottom line is that the suspect went back to jail.

That day galvanized my passion to help educate other animal control agencies about the dog fighting industry, and to collaborate with these agencies in actual investigations in order to stop this horrific "blood sport." It is dangerous work because of dog fighters' affiliation with gambling and the sale of drugs and firearms. I have become an expert witness in court against dog fighting and have participated in other "busts" against dog fighters since this initial incident.

Animal control agencies and the judicial system (including prosecutors and judges) have a long way to go before they fully understand all aspects of dog fighting and work to get these cases through the legal system as felony convictions. Detection and successful, timely prosecution of these offenders is imperative because it has been proven that people who perform animal abuse do so as a precursor to higher crimes, which can include child abuse. It is currently mandated that veterinarians are to report to law enforcement any suspected cases of animal abuse/cruelty, including dog fighting, if a patient presents to them with signs of injury consistent with these crimes. This is an important step forward because there is no doubt: lives will depend on it.

Chapter Seven:
The World of Animal Hoarders and Collectors

But They Mean Well...

Lieutenant Folsom, from the West Valley shelter, and I worked together on many kennel inspections and animal cruelty cases. But my most memorable experience was working with him on an animal collector/hoarder case where, in a single dwelling, an ACO discovered 600 dead, dying, ill, and feral (non-tame) cats. Later, we found out that we made history with that L.A. "bust." That inhumane dwelling was the largest in the history of animal collector/hoarder cases reported across the country.

But first, it is important for you to understand exactly what an animal collector or animal hoarder is. It is interesting that this classification has become disturbingly more apparent in the animal world and has become a topic of study for psychologists. Often times, these people (hoarders) fit the general description of elderly women, living alone, and usually reclusive. They have an uncontrollable habit of bringing animals, most often cats, into their home under the premise that they are rescuing them from the streets or from death in an animal shelter. Many hoarders will tell you that they are holding these animals temporarily while they find suitable adopters to take them. Therefore, in their minds, they are not only doing something good for animals, but are providing a valuable service for the community in preventing these animals from being taken into the local animal shelter.

Unfortunately, it is often the case that these women become out of control with the number of animals they continue to take in. They just can't possibly say "no" to any stray animal that comes their way. They become consumed by the tasks of daily care and sanitation that must be provided for the animals, which leaves them little, if any, time to pursue advertising these animals for adoption. Neither can they interview perspective adopters. This vicious cycle leads to animals continuing to come into, and no animals leaving, the residence. The result is an overwhelming quagmire of urine, feces, and diseased cats. The hoarder becomes overwhelmed by the daily duties and eventually gives up. The hoarder also becomes increasingly depressed and ceases to care for the animals when they suffer, so often times the animals die from starvation or disease.

Unfortunately, many of these hoarders have mental disturbances that lead them to this behavior and the habit of collection. The job of an animal control agency is to protect the public and animals, so they must investigate complaints pertaining to hoarders. Usually, animal control confiscates the animals and cares for them at the animal shelter while awaiting the completion of the legal case that is pursued against the hoarder for animal cruelty. The end result is usually that the hoarder is given conditions by the judge which outline whether or not she can own any animals currently or in the future and how many. Hoarders may be placed on probation, and animal control has the right to enter and inspect their premises at any time during this period to ensure compliance with the probationary rules pertaining to animal ownership. After the legal process is completed, the animals that were originally taken off the property by Animal Control are adopted out (if they are fit for adoption), or they may be euthanized if they are either suffering or are perhaps vicious, posing a threat to public safety.

In addition to collecting animals, hoarders usually collect other material items as well, including newspapers, clothing, and just everyday garbage. Some of these houses are so filled with garbage that the hoarder has to create a maze similar to ones you see mice running through to find the cheese. It's nearly impossible to move from room to room. The garbage forms the actual wall of the maze, and I have seen walls up to two feet in height. Now try to imagine the physical appearance of the interior of such a house, where there are over a hundred cats and piles of trash. Go a step further and use your other senses as you form this picture in your mind. Think of the smell that must be present, of urine-soaked carpeting and wood floors covered in rotting garbage. Now you are ready to read on about the L.A. "bust" of the house with over 600 feral cats.

Scoping the Problem

It all started in early July—when the temperatures had already soared, indicating that summer was here to stay in the West Valley. I was working with one of my RVTs out of the North Central shelter, and I received a 911 page from Lieutenant Folsom. I knew this had to be big because he never would page me like that erroneously. There truly was an emergency... I scrambled to a telephone and immediately was patched through to the Lieutenant.

"Hey Doc, this is big. I mean really big. It is kind of complicated though, and I can't tell you the whole thing now, but I need you to come out to the Valley. We just identified a single-family two-bedroom house with over 400 cats in it."

I winced at the other end of the phone line and said, "Oh my God."

He replied, "I know. You won't believe it, but this guy called me this morning. Evidently he had taken a few cats over to this place several weeks ago because one of his friends suggested it to him as a cat rescue house. He wasn't allowed inside, but could only drop the cats off at the door. He said he was suspicious, but he was desperate to find a place for the cats. The woman at the door said he could come back and visit them anytime he liked, but that she would try to get them adopted. So get this, the guy goes back today, and the woman won't let him in the door. So he sneeks around the back of the place, looks over the fence, sees inside, and the place is crawling with cats! I just sent one of my officers out to investigate, and he was in a panic. He radioed me from his vehicle and estimated the number to be around 400."

I too panicked for a minute, wondering where in God's name we were going to put over 400 cats in the middle of the busiest season for the shelters, the middle of Summer.

I must have been silent on the line for a few seconds too many, because I was awakened from my thoughts by Lieutenant Folsom's voice. "Doc, you still there?"

"Yes, I'm still here," I quickly answered. "What condition are the cats in?"

"The Officer said, from what he could see, there were a lot with snotty noses, and they were all housed together—the sick and the healthy lookin' ones. I'm getting my coveralls on now, and I will meet you out there. How long do you think it will take you to be there?"

"At least 45 minutes to an hour... I have to get some supplies together, and I have to organize some RVTs to go with me and some to be awaiting delivery of cats at the shelter."

"OK, I will see you there. Try to get there as fast as you can." Then the line went dead, and I knew Lieutenant Folsom probably had one leg and one arm in his coveralls while he was on the phone with me, and when he hung up, he quickly jumped into the rest of the one-piece field suit.

I hung up the phone and explained to my RVT what was happening. He immediately volunteered to go out to the Valley with me. I made a few phone calls, explained the situation to my staff, and had two additional RVTs meet me at the scene. I assigned two others to remain at the West Valley shelter. The lead RVT at the shelter would also call two to three private veterinarians in the area. We'd ask if they would come to the shelter for a few hours and assist with examining cats as they came in from the field. I spoke with the Senior ACT at the shelter and gave him a heads up. He needed to start moving animals around to make space for the incoming cats, including isolation areas for the sick.

This was a huge project considering that the shelter already was filled to capacity. We all knew that we would have to be creative to house all of these cats. I told everyone to hang tight until I could get on the scene and accurately access the health status of the animals. I also needed to get a specific total count of animals we would have to house. Everyone knew the drill because animal control probably conducted 4-5 hoarder investigations per year, involving over 100 animals per case.

The RVT I took with me had not been on the job for more than a year or so, and this was his first major hoarder case. There is no way I could prepare him for what he was about to see, so we just talked about getting our supplies together. We prepared by packing up a medical bag with stethoscopes, emergency drugs, and euthanasia solution, knowing that often times in these situations, animals can be found suffering and near death. We would need boxes of plastic gloves, surgical masks to help us endure the odor of the place, hand sanitizers, boxes of disposable hand wipes, and our knee-high rubber boots so that we could move through the house.

Since Lieutenant Folsom was in charge of collecting the animals, he would bring all of the holding cages. Hundreds of impound forms (individual cards to document the description of each animal) would also be used so that we could make an accurate count of the animals. I always brought additional bedding like towels and blankets, anticipating that there would probably be some geriatric animals on the premises that would need some special treatment. That was everything, so we climbed into my city-issued sedan and set out for the Valley.

When we turned onto the street where the house was located, I saw that, not only was Lieutenant Folsom already on the scene with two of his animal collection vehicles, but the horse trailer was also parked on the block. I wondered what the horse trailer was there for, but I needed to see the house first before I asked any other questions.

I didn't know exactly which house it was, so I parked the car, got out, and began walking up the sidewalk, following my nose knowing that it would lead me to the house. Sure enough, as I approached the house, the odor became more apparent. Once you have smelled the house of an animal hoarder, you will always be able to recognize it. It's the musty smell of a house that has been closed up for a while. Most of these places have either boarded-up or covered windows so that no one can see inside and discover the number of animals that are there. All other access to the outside is closed off, either in fear that some unwanted person will be able to enter the dwelling or that, God forbid, one of the creatures trapped inside would escape into the world.

As a result, no fresh air ever gets inside, and the entire place smells stagnant. Add to your nasal palette a combination of pungent Tomcat urine and cat feces overflowing in cat boxes and scattered all over the floors and walls. Other finds include opened cans of cat food that have been sitting out for days, rotting garbage throughout, and the occasional decaying body of a cat that is now being cannibalized by the trapped survivors. This is what you smell, and not just for the time you are in the house. When you go home that night, no matter how many times you wash your hair, there is still a faint hint of that odor. You don't dare bring your hosed off boots anywhere near your house. They either stay outside your garage or in your trunk awaiting the next investigation. This house fulfilled this description of odors and even surpassed our wildest dreams. I have never to this day seen anything quite like the interior of this house.

The Plan of Action

Because the odor began to overpower me as I stood on the sidewalk, I knew to walk up that particular driveway. I was right. Inside a porch area that was partitioned off from public view, I met up with Lieutenant Folsom. He was standing among bags and cases of cat food piled high. He was expertly directing the investigation team of animal control officers (at least seven in my view), as well as ACTs working on collecting the animals. As I expected, he had everything organized, he had already assessed the situation, he'd determined the plan of action, and he had everyone working like a fine-tuned clock.

He looked at me and smiled. "You think you're ready for this one?"

"I don't know. How bad is it?" I asked.

"Well, the initial officer underestimated a bit. I think we are closer to 500 cats, and most of them are feral, so they are having a devil of a time collecting them. I brought the horse trailer over too so that we could load cat carriers and cages into it and transport them back to the shelter that way. Otherwise, we will be here all day and night moving these animals in the six-compartment collection vehicles."

I took a deep breath, purposefully exhaled loudly, and put my right palm to my forehead, which had started to pound. It was about 2:00 P.M. in the afternoon, and I knew we would definitely be here all day and probably into the night, just collecting these animals and sending them through medical processing. "Where is the person responsible for all of these cats?" I asked.

"She just left in a police vehicle after they placed her under arrest. But it's more complicated than that. She's a rescue 'friend' with the department and knows the General Manager." He put his head down and shook it from side to side. "There is going to be trouble on this one."

During the late 1990's, the common way to handle a hoarding situation was to arrest the hoarder. Because medical professionals began to study and learn more about all forms of hoarding, it is now handled as a psychological condition.

I boldly moved forward past the hustle and bustle of the staff. They were bringing cats out in carriers to the area where vehicles were parked, and cats were being booked in, or "impounded." I entered the house and was set aback, not only by the heat (which had to be close to 100 degrees in this house that didn't have air conditioning) but also by the smell of ammonia from cat urine. The hairs inside my nose began to twitch, and then I felt the burning set in. I looked up and passed a female news reporter who was being escorted off the property by the department's public information officer. She'd wanted to see the house for herself in order to do some accurate reporting. It seemed like she couldn't get out of that house fast enough. She whisked by me with a handkerchief over her nose and mouth, clearly hoping that it would assist her current state of labored breathing until she found refuge on the sidewalk in the fresh air.

I looked around on the floor of the house, and for a split second, I felt dizzy, like I had lost my balance. It appeared that the floor was moving and I was sure I was about ready to faint due to the ammonia smell, but as I looked more closely, in fact the floor *was* moving. Every square inch of the floor was covered by cats. You could not see the actual floor. As they scurried around, desperately trying to find a hiding place due to all of the strangers in the house, I could catch only brief glimpses of linoleum. When I did, I saw it was streaked brown with feces, cat food, and a layer of garbage—newspapers, dry cat food bags, and fast food containers. (At times like this, you are extremely thankful that someone designed knee-high rubber protective boots...)

As I walked through the entry and entered the living room, it was like wading through a shallow pool of water, except here, the water was replaced by moving cats. Each step seemed like it was in slow motion, similar to how water holds you back when you try to walk through it. There was evidence of some furniture. A sofa in the middle of the room was covered with cat hair, about three inches thick, embedded into the fabric. I watched an animal control officer move the sofa over. About ten cats ran from underneath it, searching for a new hiding place. But as I took a closer look under the sofa, I saw the remains of the front half of a cat carcass that these cats had been feeding on in order to stay alive. I thought this had to be the worst of it, and I continued on.

I walked into the bedroom, or what I assumed used to be a bedroom because there was a bed in it, so filthy and covered with animals and garbage that you couldn't and wouldn't even sit on it, let alone lie down on it for any reason. There was a dresser of drawers that could hardly be seen from underneath the piled garbage in the room. I had not touched anything in the house as of yet, but for some reason, I was drawn to that dresser, and something inside me told me I had to open those drawers. I took the plastic gloves from the back pocket of my blue uniform pants and quickly placed them on each hand. Once I secured them in place, their tight fit would allow me to handle things without any fear of contamination through them.

I moved toward the dresser and reached out for the top drawer. I hesitated to open it, but I grabbed the crusty knob and dragged the drawer open. Nothing but dirt—I was relieved. I reached for the second one and cautiously opened it. As I pulled open the drawer, out popped the head of a weak, dehydrated adult cat. She cried quietly, and her eyes squinted in the dim light of the bedroom.

"Jesus Christ," I hollered.

My frustration had reached its limit with this situation and this "rescue" person. This was the worst case of animal cruelty I had ever faced. I grabbed the animal from the drawer. Her body lay limp in my arms, and her breathing was agonal. How long had she been suffering, stuffed in this drawer, starving to death? She was dying before my eyes, and I could not allow her to suffer any longer.

I quickly carried her out of the noxious fumes of the house into the front driveway where I'd left my medical bag at the medical station we had set up there. I set her on the ground on a blanket in the fresh air. I reached for her pulse. It was weak and thready, and her eyes started to roll back in her head. I quickly opened the medical bag and searched for the euthanasia solution and a needle and syringe. I drew up a small amount of the blue fluid and slowly approached her as she lay listless on the ground beside me. One of the ACTs came up to me and offered assistance. He quickly completed an impound card on the cat, documenting the general description of the animal, and assigned it an impound number. I knelt down and quietly assured her that she would no longer have to suffer in this terrible world. As officers continued to hurry by, focused on their job at hand, the three of us, my ACT assistant, this small cat, and I were in a world of our own. I injected her and then held her while I felt her take her last breath. She was finally at peace.

I carried her out to the front where the cat cages and carriers were and discovered she was one of about ten other cats that had been found dead on the premises and were being identified and tagged. I placed her with the others. As I made my way back to the house, I looked up, and a few feet from the house down the sidewalk, I saw 5-6 people I recognized as local animal activists from the community. I was sure they were there in support of us removing the animals from these awful conditions. But when I looked their way, they caught my stare and started shouting, "There she is, Dr. Death. How many of these innocent animals are you going to kill today?"

I was shocked by their comments. I was still mentally getting over what I had just seen in that house, and now I had to face these illogical and uninformed people. I walked over to them and asked them to follow me. They did, and I led them to the now ten dead bodies that were lying on the grassy hill at the entrance to the house. I said to them, "All of these animals were found either dead or dying in this house due to lack of care. What would you say if I ran my animal shelters like this and allowed this to happen?" I wanted them to take a quick trip into reality.

One particularly aggressive woman responded, "This happens sometimes in a sanctuary. She just wanted to help them. She would never kill them like you do."

And there I had the explanation. It didn't matter what we did as the Department of Animal Control, or what the hoarder did. The hoarder would always be justified in their minds for his or her actions, and even for animal care so irresponsible that it could be termed animal cruelty. I knew from that moment on that reason and logic would not be of any help to me. No matter what heroic acts we performed, regardless of how many animals we relieved from suffering, we would always be the "bad guys" in the minds of these unstable people. I moved away from them and continued on with the horrendous task that lay before me.

Catch Poles and Cages

I re-entered the house and moved to the back rear bedroom where two officers were trying to catch these wild cats. I made the mistake of opening the closed door, and at that very moment, several cats whizzed by my head at lightning speed like they were flying. One of the officers shouted at me to close the door. I did immediately and entered the room. I saw that both officers had "catch poles" in their hands and were trying to restrain the cats long enough to safely place them in transport cages.

Many people and agencies don't believe in using a catch pole (sometimes called a "rabies pole") on a cat. This device is a long steel pole with a wire loop at the end. The diameter of the loop is controlled by the handler of the pole, and it can be expanded and shortened as needed in order to fit around the neck of an animal. The pole is used when the animal can't be controlled safely by a rope lead or herded into a cage. The stiffness of the steel pole allows the handler to keep the animal a safe distance away from his/her body so that the handler is not injured by the jaws or claws of a fractious (difficult to handle/aggressive) animal. ACOs and kennel staff require training and a lot of practice to become proficient and humane at handling this piece of equipment.

Many people don't believe that this device can be or should be used on cats because they have a different physical shape compared to the stout body of a dog. It is thought that other restraint devices such as thick leather gloves and bags can be used to restrain hard-to-handle, especially-feral cats. I think that all of these types of equipment have their place in a large housing facility for animals. But given the situation we were faced with, an open area like a house and the sheer number of animals to catch, there was no way that anything but poles could be used to collect these animals. They were literally springing off the walls, the ceiling, and occasionally, if we came within close enough distance to them, our bodies as well.

If we had used another form of restraint, which would have necessitated that the officers come in close contact with the cats, we would have risked injury to every handler, and imposed tremendous stress on each animal, as the actual collection time would double or triple. Because a cat bite is second only to a human bite in causing severe infection, we weighed the consequences. We wanted to cause the least amount of stress to these cats and collect them with the least amount of handling in the fastest way possible. Our only alternative was the "catch pole."

It was fascinating to watch these officers handle this situation and see how they controlled their catch poles. Their arms and these poles became fluid in motion, moving as one entity. In this particular room, the officers were all set up to enhance their efficiency, just as Lieutenant Folsom had trained them. The transfer cages used for the cats were smaller metal cages with a sliding, guillotine door on the front of the cage that could be closed quickly once the animal was placed in the cage. There is quite a difference between placing a tame cat in a cage and convincing a wild or feral cat that it needs to be in a cage. The transfer cages were set up on one side of the room, and cats were herded to the other side. Otherwise, they would be constantly knocking everything down and possibly injuring themselves.

The cages were set on end, so when the guillotine doors were raised awaiting a new resident, they were pulled out horizontally rather than vertically as in a normal resting position. Once an officer successfully looped a cat at the end of the pole, the officer would try to control the animal's body movement. The objective was to keep the cat on the end of the pole for the least amount of time. The officer would then lift the cat from the floor and pour it into the upright cage. Using a boot-covered foot, the officer would steady the cage and semi-cover the door's opening while reaching back with a glove-protected hand to slide the guillotine door closed. Just before the door was completely closed, the officer would release the loop at the end of the pole, and the cat would quickly slip its head from the control of the pole.

From that point onward, the cat was free to use its claws and teeth with more accuracy from within the cage to attack any person who was careless enough to come anywhere near the cage without protection. Once the cat was secure in the cage, the cage would be placed back in an upright position, and the caged cats were placed together at one end of the room. When between 8-10 cats were collected, a kennel person would come in and carry the cages to the outdoor impound area. Each cat would receive an impound number and card with a description of the animal and then be placed in a transport vehicle to go back to the shelter for further examination and housing. During this process, either myself or one of the RVTs would treat cats that required immediate medical attention on site.

As you can imagine, feral cats do not want to be restricted in their movement or contained in any way. Their instinct is to hide from human beings for safety and survival. Being placed in a cage makes them extremely uncomfortable, and some will go to great lengths to escape the confines of the cage. Often times, shelter employees will receive cats in traps at the shelter. The general public will bring in cats this way. I saw many of these cats come in with severe head trauma, lacerations on their foreheads, and swollen eyes and cheeks. One of the kennel staff once said to me, "You really know when it's a feral cat in one of these traps, and not someone's pet, when you see how they beat themselves up in the trap." I came to know through experience that a person's pet may be scared in the trap and hide in the back of the cage, but it won't relentlessly pound its head against the cage, trying to break free, for hours upon end.

The cats we were collecting out of the house were no different. Many would relentlessly try to free themselves from the transport cages and would severely injure their heads. We would try to calm them down by covering their cages with towels so they felt more inconspicuous and safe. Sometimes it helped. Sometimes it did not. It also was problematic when we tried to treat these injured animals because one could never safely handle them to examine them, let alone to clean up and place topical medication on their wounds. By the end of the day, it ended up being the case that around 90 percent of the cats we collected that day were feral cats and probably unadoptable.

As the afternoon wore on, the ambient temperature in the house began to rise, and within a few hours, the officers were dripping with sweat in this enclosed space and suffocating from the strong fumes. They took frequent breaks outside in the fresh air and then went back in to collect ten or more cats at a time.

I stepped back outside and checked the impound area where the entire horse trailer was now filled with cat transport cages. I knew that we had to change our plan of action for housing these guys. I would have to enlist support from the remaining five shelters. Generally, it was the responsibility of the shelter in the district from which the investigation originated to take on any further housing responsibilities. However, over the past five years or so, these hoarder cases had come to involve so many animals that it had become a multi-district problem. I can't imagine what other agencies do that have only one shelter and no other options for holding animals.

Isolating the Sick Cats

The answer to the question of where we were going to individually house these animals actually ended up being a simple one. I alerted all shelters that we would not euthanize other animals in the shelter to make holding space for these cats—cats that appeared at this time to be unadoptable. But I still wanted to give these animals a chance to calm down after this traumatic day so we could see which ones might end up being handled and possibly adopted. I also knew by looking at the condition of the cats—many with noses draining green snot, open-mouthed breathing, and emaciated bodies—that a large percentage would probably have to be euthanized. Not only did I have to think of these animals, but the potential for disease transmission throughout the shelter once these animals were housed there became a legitimate concern. We would have to figure out a way to group-house these animals, rather than house them individually, in order to save valuable cage space. I contacted the Senior ACTs at each shelter, planted the seed for them to figure out how to group-house these animals, and started transporting hundreds of cats all over the city to each shelter.

As I left the holding area and was heading back up to the house, I saw some cats separated from the rest in carriers, not our transport cages, that were very ill, and I stopped to take a look at them. One of the officers who was securing the area pulled me aside. "Hey, Doc, you won't believe this," he said. "See that lady over there with the brown hair and the ponytail?" I nodded. "She was actually living in that house with all of those cats in all that crap. She was the caretaker for the lady who owned the place, the one that we arrested. See those cats in the carriers? We found them in the house, trapped in those carriers on heating pads."

I was appalled. It must have been over 95 degrees in that house. What would possess this woman to put these adult cats on heating pads and literally cook them?

The officer continued. "She said the vet told her, since they were sick, to keep them warm, and they would be all right. And she is supposed to care for animals? I tell you, Doc, each time I go on one of these cases, I become more and more negative against mankind."

This was unbelievable, and I just had to find out for myself what made this woman tick, so I approached her myself. As I walked up to her, the first thing I took note of was the overpowering smell of male cat urine. I noticed she was in her early 50's, filthy, with pink pants on, and a smock top for which I couldn't really identify the original color because the top was covered with stains. My eyes ended up at her feet. I noticed she was wearing open-toed, torn-up sandals. Her feet were streaked with dirt and presumably feces. Her toenails were so badly overgrown that they passed the tip of her sandals. Dirt and other dark material had accumulated beneath all of her nails, and I wondered when the last time was that those feet had ever been cleaned.

Interestingly enough, I've come to recognize animal hoarders by making some simple, albeit unscientific, observations when they are out in public. Each one that I have encountered has been a woman for starters. The smell of their cat-urine-soaked clothes is the first tip off. Add to that their overall attire (always stained and filthy, and the clothing design most commonly is a moo-moo). Finally there is the poor hygienic condition of their feet (usually on display through open-toed shoes). So what I was seeing seemed typical.

Before I said a word to her, I wondered how anyone could move through the layers of feces and garbage in that house with open toed shoes. I also wondered where she rested her body in that quagmire, whether it be in a sitting position or lying down?

I introduced myself to her and asked her about the conditions of the cats in the carriers that surrounded her. She responded in a frustrated tone. "The vet told me to keep these here cats in carriers. When they get sick like this, I keep 'em warm, just like he told me."

I couldn't contain myself and had to ask her, "Did he tell you to keep them on heating pads when the temperature in your house was over 95 degrees?"

She confidently responded, "We don't have the money to take all of these sick cats to the vet. I know what they got, and I just keep 'em warm and give them those antebeotics when I can, and they all gonna get better."

At that point, that was all that I could take from her, and I promptly walked away. I then indicated to one of the kennel staff that all of the cats in the carriers needed to be isolated for upper respiratory illness and would be housed separately at the shelter. Next I tried to locate Lieutenant Folsom and tell him the unbelievable story I had just heard.

I found him with several of the officers, setting up the transport schedule and simultaneously talking on the radio. Before I could finish my story of the cats in carriers on heating pads, he interrupted me and let me know his new finding. He said that, at the time that the citizen observed the interior of the house, some of the cats were housed in large pens. When the officer arrived to assess the situation before we all arrived, he reported those pens were open, and the cats housed there were moving freely among the general population of cats in the house. When Lieutenant Folsom interviewed the live-in caretaker, she said that the sick cats were in those pens, but she let them all out before we came. I looked up to the sky in horror because that meant that now all of the cats in the house had been thoroughly exposed to these sick cats and every one would have to be isolated. We would just have to set up different levels of isolation based on the clinical presentation of the animals.

Facing Horrors... Housing Victims...

I needed to return back into the house to finish my observations of all of the rooms and conditions these animals were in. As I walked through the living room area, I saw that the officers had been working hard and had collected about 70 percent of the cats in this area. I made my way to the bathroom, and a new horror met me there. There were litter boxes actually set up throughout the house, but in the bathroom, there were about six of them. I can't imagine the last time they were scooped, let alone the litter changed in them. They were overflowing with mounds of feces piled upon each other. The sink area had streaks of feces, probably wiped off from the paws of the cats who attempted to use the overfilled litter boxes. The tub was no different, except that the cats had started using the tub as a urine marking box, and spray marks of Tom cat urine were evident throughout.

The toilet was not functioning, and I was told there was something wrong with the plumbing. It appeared that the human dwellers were also utilizing an area near the tub to take care of their personal calling for daily elimination. The coving along the wall perimeter was covered in dirt and debris that appeared to be flush with the wall. Evidence of some past human use of this room could be seen by the presence of a filthy plastic cup by the faucet, presumably used to rinse one's mouth after brushing teeth. This, too, must have been an activity that took place a long time ago. There was no evidence that the live-in caretaker was practicing any level of hygiene now. The smell was so all-consuming that my eyes were burning behind my gas permeable contacts. I didn't dare touch my face or my eyes, so the only relief was to just allow my eyes to tear up in an attempt to rinse some of the irritants from them. I looked behind the toilet and saw two cats huddled up together, sitting as still as possible, hoping to be missed in the middle of all of the confusion. My body began to protest against the filth, and I had the feeling I might unexpectedly retch, so I quickly left the room.

It was now around 6:00 P.M., we had been on the scene for over four hours, and the collection process wasn't even halfway completed. The first group of transport vehicles had left the location in order to deliver animals, and their first stop was to the West Valley shelter. I was paged by the Senior ACT at the shelter who told me over the phone that his holding areas were full and that we would have to dispatch the remaining transport vehicles to the other shelters. So we started organizing.

I contacted Jane at East Valley who was willing to stay and examine and house all cats we delivered her way. The Senior ACT and the RVT at North Central had a brilliant idea, and they were working on converting the barn used for large animals into an open holding area for the cats. They were working on securing it so that no cats would escape, and they estimated that they could possibly hold 150-200 cats in that area without disturbing or exposing their stray cat population. The South L.A. shelter was also ready, and they were converting their former spay/neuter clinic that had about 50 holding cages in it into an isolation ward for these cats. That was about it. Four of the shelters had the capacity to take in these extra cats. What a team to all pitch in and make this work... They didn't scoff about the hardship it would place on them to care for an additional 100-200 animals per day. They just "took care of business."

The biggest question about these cases soon becomes the length of time the shelters will be holding these animals. It is not uncommon for a humane investigation to be ongoing for months and sometimes even up to a year. With this number of animals in our possession, we were in a state of emergency, and I hoped Lieutenant Folsom could work some magic to put this case on the fast track. We would only be able to wait and see.

Fortunately, the sunlight stayed with us until after 8:30 P.M., and everyone was still catching and placing in transport cages cats, more cats, and even more cats. The investigation team was exhausted, and even Lieutenant Folsom was growing weary. He told me the current count was well over 500 at this point, and he estimated that we would hit the 600 mark before all of the work was done. He also mentioned that they wouldn't be leaving until all of the cats were caught. He did bring in some relief officers and sent some officers home, but most wanted to stay and finish the job. Most of the cats that needed immediate emergency triage had been removed from the house, and the fastest, best hiders remained for the officers to retrieve. These cats were challenging and were going to take a great deal of time to catch. It was now time for me to report to the shelters and assist with further examination of cats as well as placement. I told Lieutenant Folsom that I would be out at West Valley and would meet him there later.

As I drove to the shelter, I finally realized how hungry I was. But at the same time, I continued to have subliminal flashes in my brain of the poorest sanitation I had ever been exposed to, and the thought of eating also made me sick to my stomach. I phoned the West Valley Shelter from my car and asked the ACT to call in for about eight large pizzas. I said I'd be there in time to pay for it. The folks at the shelters had also been on duty for about fourteen hours and everyone needed a little fuel.

When I arrived at the shelter, I drove around to the back parking lot and headed for the loading dock, which was adjacent to the euthanasia room. I got out of my car and paused for a minute, taking in the sweet smell of the bales of hay and alfalfa that were on hand to feed the large animals housed there. I then entered the euthanasia room from the rear entrance.

The Mad-house at the Shelter

The room was filled with transport cages of cats lined up and piled on top of each other. I walked out of the room, and the entire corridor had cages against the walls filled with cats that were whining, meowing, spitting, and exuding nasal discharge. The odor of the house had permeated the haircoats of these animals, and now the entire West Valley shelter had taken on the odor of that wretched house. That was another problem we faced when taking in animals from a hoarder's house. Unless you thoroughly or repeat-bathed the animals housed there, that smell infused the new holding area. I knew we were not going to entertain the idea of bathing any cats, especially feral ones, so I guess we and the public would have to endure this rank smell for a while.

I looked up, and one of my RVTs, Palo, who was a foreign veterinarian licensed to practice in India, approached me. He was very articulate, well-educated, organized, and very business-oriented. "Doctor Dena, this is a mad house. I am working with Dr. Orsted. He has been here with his technician examining cats with me for over the past several hours."

"Let's go find them," I replied. "I need to thank them for all of their hard work."

We walked down the hallway and to the outside where even more cats were in cages. Dr. Orsted was also a foreign veterinarian who had obtained his license here in the states and had always been helpful and supportive of the shelters. I knew when I saw him that he was exhausted, so I thanked him and his technician for their assistance and sent them home for food and rest. They offered to come back in the morning to help, and I wearily agreed.

Palo and I marched back to the euthanasia room and began examining cats. He told me that only about 15 of the cats they examined so far were tame. The rest were feral and would not tolerate being handled. He commented in a quiet voice, "You know, Doctor Dena, many of these cats are very sick, and we must consider euthanasia."

"I know," I said. "Let's start making some decisions."

Cats didn't look like individuals to me anymore. There were hundreds of short-haired, silver tabbies and double that number of all "black" cats. Most of the cats were examined through the cage. There just was no way they would tolerate us near them, and at our level of exhaustion, it was certain that we would be injured by them.

Just because animals can't talk our language, doesn't mean you can't observe physical signs in them that tell you they are not feeling well. Especially with cats, who are usually fastidious about cleanliness and grooming... If they stop attending to their general appearance, this is one of the first signs that something is wrong.

The sick cats I was faced with sat in their transport cages in a characteristic position. It identified that they were struggling to breathe. They had their elbows tucked into their sides, and their heads held low, and were even occasionally nodding. The discharge from their nostrils extended all the way to the floor of the cage, creating two vertical lines of a sticky, gooey material from their noses. Some of their eyes were caked closed with discharge, while others had corneal ulcers that were obviously painful as they squinted to look at me through the red, irritated sclera (white portion of the eye). Many of them had diarrhea adhered to the hair surrounding their rectum. Their hair coats looked greasy and ungroomed. In sum, many of these cats appeared to have given up the fight.

Palo and I examined about thirty cats through about 10:30 P.M. We had separated cats into three categories: those that appeared healthy, those that were sick and in need of medication and isolation, and those for whom euthanasia would be a mercy. I looked at Palo, and he knew what I was asking. "Don't worry, Doc. I will take care of the euthanasias. There is really nothing you can do for them now. Don't feel badly," he said, trying to console me at the end of a very long day.

We did a bit more organizing of housing space. We felt badly that the graveyard shift ACT (midnight to 8:00 A.M.) would have plenty to do this evening and would be shocked when he walked in. I knew that staff had everything under control at this point, and that I would have an equally long day tomorrow, traveling to the other locations to examine cats and housing, so I had to get home and try to get some sleep. I got in my car and actually appreciated the hour-long drive as I reviewed the events of the day in my mind. As I turned off on my exit in Long Beach and drove through the neighborhoods to my home, it was one of those times when I had no idea how I had gotten there. I guessed by now, my city vehicle actually did know the way home by itself.

Caring For All the New Residents

I looked at my wristwatch, it was after midnight, and I still had to shower and spend a little time with my animals. I pulled into my driveway, got out of the car, and thankfully smelled the clean air with traces of an ocean breeze. I grabbed my knee-high rubber boots (I had sprayed them down back at the shelter...) and placed them outside in the side yard to air out (if that was possible). I walked into a dark house and was thankful my sister was living with me at the time. She had fed and cared for my dogs and cats while I was gone. My husband was in Sacramento, and with the day- and night-long investigation, I missed our evening phone call. I would have much to tell him tomorrow evening.

I dragged my body into the shower and soaped up at least twice that I remember. I used the most fragrant body wash and shampoo I could find. I toweled off and covered myself in powder and perfume. My dogs came running out of my bedroom followed by my sister, quite anxious to see me.

"You guys have been all over the news tonight," she said as I watched her nose turn up a little. "Did you already shower?" she asked.

"Yes," I answered. "But you can still smell me, can't you?"

"It's not too bad," she said.

I looked up, and both dogs had already found their places on my bed. They were cuddled up in the sheets, waiting for me to join them.

"Do you want me to bring the cats in too?" my sister asked.

"No," I said. "Why don't you keep them in your room for tonight."

Over the next several days, I traveled from shelter to shelter to work with staff on isolation housing and customized methods for medicating all of the sick cats. As I mentioned earlier, Brea and Vince set up a unique housing situation at the North Central shelter. When they took me out to the barn area, despite the lingering smell of the hoarder house, I was pleasantly surprised to see about 150-200 of the cats comfortably spread out throughout the indoor barn. Brea had even rigged a secure "sunning" area for the cats. It served the secondary purpose of providing fresh air to the barn because she was able to open a back doorway that faced the shelter's rear entrance, behind our security gates. Vince motioned for me to look overhead, and as my gaze followed the side walls of the barn up to the ceiling, I saw cats hanging out in the rafters, lined up for the length of the beam. They were everywhere in the barn, but they were all much more comfortable than in individual cages. I knew the fresh air would also do them some good.

Vince said, "Most of them are sick, and we can't catch them twice a day to medicate them. It is already taking a lot of manpower to empty all of the litter boxes we have spread out all over the barn."

I looked around and got an idea. "What if we fed them in the big troughs and laced the food with antibiotics? Since we know most are sick and all the rest have been exposed to illness, it will be sort of a combined treatment and preventive program."

Brea said, "That will make it much easier on the kennel staff. We will just need Vince to mix in the medication."

And so it went... About 200 feral cats got better and did so faster than at any of our other facilities. Soon after we impounded all of the cats, the court made a ruling that none of them would be returned to the rescuer that owned the house. We started reaching out to local and national feral cat organizations, to see if they had sanctuaries that had room to take some of our population. These groups really stepped up and ended up placing around fifty percent of the cats all over the country. Some of the kitties actually calmed down over time, and with daily interaction by the kennel staff, could actually be handled and were adopted. Others did not respond to treatment and were humanely euthanized.

I was so proud of our staff for their compassion and the level of care we provided for these cats—cats that, for no fault of their own, became the victims of a rescue situation that had turned into a hoarding situation. According to the housing authority, the hoarder's house was deemed uninhabitable and was gutted. Those that survived this tragedy were now calling new places—home.

Chapter Eight:
The World of Animal Rescue—Friend or Foe?

Despite the fact that it is not politically correct to say so, there can be a love/hate relationship between animal rescue groups and animal control. Unless you are actively in the animal sheltering world, you probably can't imagine why these two entities might butt heads.

Let's take it from the point of view of an animal control employee. For starters, the word "rescue"... The foundation of many rescue groups is that they "rescue" animals from the shelter. Just think about that for a minute. That insinuates that it is so horrible at the animal shelter that the animals must be rescued from it. This view is usually propagated to potential adopters from rescue organizations to help facilitate an adoption and/or obtain a donation.

Stray animals roaming the streets are picked up by an animal control officer and placed in a shelter environment with clean and dry housing, food, water, and medical care. That certainly sounds like a "rescue" situation to me. I have always thought the rescue groups should respectfully be referred to as Rescue Partners with sheltering agencies. They support the rescue work the shelter has started by creating a third outlet for stray animals. The first and second possible dispositions for shelter animals are either adoption or being reclaimed by an owner. The reality of the "stray" situation is that animal control actually serves as the Agency of Rescue for stray and lost animals.

The concept that rescue groups are rescuing shelter animals from euthanasia also serves to paint animal control as the "bad guys." Again, the reality of the situation is that most rescue groups are not taking the least adoptable animals (large-sized breeds, animals that are black in color, geriatric animals, pit bulls or pit bull mixed breeds, shy or aggressive animals, etc.). These animals are the ones more likely to be euthanized due to lack of adopter interest or temperament issues. Most rescuers are looking for the most adoptable animals (smaller breeds, cute and/or fluffy creatures, animals that are white in color, animals with friendly temperaments, etc.). Rescuers also selectively take purebred animals from the shelter because they know they can turn those adoptions around faster, which means less extraneous investment for food and housing while they wait for an interested adopter.

So when this scenario continually plays out at a shelter, you will see a reduction in the number of the most adoptable animals available for the public, and the remaining animals usually take longer to be placed in homes. Everything has a domino effect, and this is no exception. Each extra day an animal stays at the shelter, it is taking up space that another stray could be filling. So when animals are held for longer periods of time at a public shelter, and the daily intake of new animals continues like a running faucet, the population grows faster than the space that is available. Since all shelters are trying to minimize the number of euthanasias, the only way to do it in this scenario is to "pack them in." That means a kennel run constructed to house one to two dogs now houses four to six dogs.

So these less adoptable dogs not taken by rescue groups continue to take up space and contribute to overcrowding, but now an additional factor comes into play. The high stress suffered by animals in group housing such as in shelters is a contributing factor to lowering their immune response to disease. Couple that with the fact that many new incoming dogs may be harboring disease and are placed in kennels with these less adoptable dogs. Not only are they in close proximity to each other to transmit disease, but all of the dogs in each kennel share food and water bowls, making disease transmission quite easy through saliva and nasal discharge.

How can you possibly prevent disease in this scenario? But the choice is either house them in this manner—trying to catch disease transmitters early, treat those that are ill, and hopefully adopt them out before they become ill—or lower the shelter population so there is less illness. But ultimately (usually every couple of days), the numbers catch up with you, and the only way to make room when animals aren't adopted, rescue groups aren't interested in them, and you don't have space to house them is to euthanize. Many of you may say just increase the number of dogs housed per kennel. Unfortunately, this leads to even greater disease transmission. And the other huge obstacle is fighting between these dogs trapped in a small kennel space.

Many shelters do not have twenty-four hour staffing to monitor such a high number of animals—a number that can grow exponentially. This can result in a horrific scenario, one that is not uncommon when the population in a shelter exceeds the animal holding capacity. When staff reports in for the morning shift (and there has not been a night shift on duty) they often will find injured and even dead animals in kennels. The laws of survival of the fittest come into play. That is no way to run a shelter. So there must be a limit to the number of dogs housed per kennel. Again we have arrived at the unwelcome reality of the overpopulation story.

However, the story doesn't end there. Private rescue groups that work with governmentally operated sheltering agencies must register their organization with them, provide proof of their non-profit status, and in many communities, agree to routine facility inspections to ensure compliance with local ordinances. The reason for inspections is evident as you read the chapter on animal hoarders. It illustrates how animal rescuers who meant well when they started out can quickly become hoarders whose animals are living in squalor. This situation now becomes an animal abuse/cruelty situation. Now animal control officers must come in to rescue these animals. So ironically, the animals that were initially removed from the shelter by the rescue group to prevent overpopulation and euthanasias now return to the shelter. If the shelter doesn't have space to hold them, animals in the current shelter population that have not been adopted and have gone way past their legal holding period may have to be euthanized in order to hold the animals from the hoarding case. The tragic story comes full circle.

I have spent a lot of time explaining to you what devastating choices staff at an animal control shelter have to make on a daily basis. I also have compassion for the rescue groups that face some similar issues. They too have limited holding space and often ask the shelter to hold onto animals for extra days so that they can find a place for them (which may include recruiting a foster home). This becomes a delicate balance, and I know from experience that most kennel managers do everything in their power to hold animals for rescue groups. Unfortunately, since animal control is mandated to accept every animal that comes to the front door, they can't always extend the holding period for the amount of time a rescue group might need.

I have witnessed the agonizing decisions these kennel managers must make when contacting a rescuer to tell them that they desperately need space and can't continue to hold an animal for additional days. Sometimes a rescue group can come in and adopt the animal. Other times they just can't. Most of the rescuers that I worked with in Los Angeles had compassion for the animals but also deeply respected the pain that the kennel supervisors endured every day. They were realists who knew that not every adoption would work out. I hope now you too can understand the stress of this situation and know that the shelter and rescue groups are equally making their best efforts to save animals. Every single day, animal control employees, rescue groups, and the public must work towards treating each other with respect and compassion, with the unifying goal of adopting as many animals as possible into loving, forever-homes.

With that background, I want to introduce to you some of the wonderful animal rescue groups in the City of Los Angeles. I send them all a personal thank you for their devotion, and I hope my tribute to them serves to honor the work that they do.

The Amanda Foundation
351 North Foothill Rd.
Beverly Hills, CA 90210
(310)278-2935

At Amanda, love never strays. "Amanda" means worthy of love. The Foundation is located in Beverly Hills and is a 501(c)(3) non-profit organization. They rescue animals from Los Angeles City and County shelters and provide adoption services for dogs, cats, puppies, and kittens. They also operate a full-service veterinary practice and operate a Spaymobile.

There is a great deal of wealth in Los Angeles, and some of the rescue groups are very well-funded by loyal donors. They contribute to the foundations to promote projects such as building state of the art holding facilities and purchasing mobile spay/neuter clinics. During my first year with animal control, I met a woman from one of these organizations at the North Central Shelter. She was meticulously walking through the kennels and making a list of about 12-15 dogs she was preparing to adopt on behalf of her organization. She looked familiar to me, and staff told me that she was a former actress and her name was Teri Austin. Later I found out she was a Canadian-born actress that appeared on the popular television show *Knots Landing* as Jill Bennett in the late 1980's. Others may recognize her for her work in the crime drama *Matlock*. I asked the kennel staff if this was the average number of dogs she would take as I was impressed with these large numbers. They told me she came in about every other week and sometimes would take even more dogs. It all depended on how many adoptions the Foundation completed and what their available holding space was at the time.

Some rescue groups come into shelters and only pick the most adoptable animals as I described previously because they can adopt them out quickly. The Amanda Foundation was different. Of course they took many small breeds, but often, they took older dogs or shy dogs that might need a little extra care to ensure proper placement. Terry understood all of the reasons why it was important to allow the shelter to also provide very adoptable animals to the public. I always had such great respect for Terry and the Amanda Foundation, not only for their commitment to the stray animals of the city, but also for their commitment to and support of the shelter.

Terry was very attractive and assertive and a powerful spokeswoman for the Foundation. Even though she was an actress, she didn't want to overwhelm shelter staff, so she never wore makeup during her adoption visits. She did, however, expect nothing less than complete organization and efficiency from us. (Considering all of the animals she took out on behalf of the Organization, she deserved it.) After she'd spent several hours picking out dogs for adoption, she did not tolerate glitches in an animal's paperwork, and she was given priority at the clerical desk when checking out and purchasing animals, which she greatly appreciated. She could have been our worst nightmare if we'd exhibited incompetence, and it was fair to say many kennel attendants ran the opposite direction when she entered the shelter due to her high expectations, but she had her favorite kennel workers, and they gladly partnered with her, knowing she was helping save lives that day.

Terry and I got along very well, and we developed a trust in each other. She would contact me to discuss holding periods or health status of different dogs from many of our shelters when an adoption had extenuating circumstances. Since I traveled to the shelters on a regular basis, I could recall many of the dogs from my visits, which improved efficiency during my follow-up with kennel supervisors on her behalf and helped validate to her that we considered these animals much more than impound numbers.

She was also a regular attendee at our City Commission Meetings and often times spoke out about pending issues at the shelter. She was tough on us when we needed it, but more often she stood up for us, not only as an agency, but she also gave praise to individual employees whenever they went above and beyond the call of duty to help her help the animals. She made us better at our job.

Her passion for her work never wavered. To this day she is still fighting for the animals in the city by efficiently operating the Foundation's mobile spay/neuter van. It travels to low socioeconomic areas of the city, providing surgical services at a low cost to pet owners. She is a superstar contributor to ending pet overpopulation in Los Angeles, and she will forever be a hero in my eyes.

The Ark Trust, Inc.
The Humane Society of the United States
Hollywood Office
820 Moraga Drive
Los Angeles, CA 90049

The Ark Trust merged with the Humane Society of the United States to become the Humane Society of the United States, Hollywood Office. Gretchen Wyler created the idea of the Genesis Awards, starting in 1986, and she continued with the annual tradition in 1991 when she founded The Ark Trust, Inc. The awards event honors members of the media that highlighted animal issues, thus increasing public awareness and compassion toward animals.

Los Angeles is not only a city filled with adventure, it's one that most importantly contains colorful characters. My ultimate favorite personality in the City of Los Angeles had to be Gretchen Wyler. She started her career as an actress and Broadway star in New York, and although she always remained a "star," she became an extraordinary animal advocate. I can't say I remember exactly the first day we met, but for me it was love at first sight. She was one of the most awe-inspiring women I have ever met.

First of all, no matter where you were or what level of conversation you were in with her, it was like visualizing a fine-tuned performance. Her body language and her emphasis of particular syllables as she spoke was masterful. Her greeting commonly used the word "Darling" with a distinct richness of tone. I know she greeted everyone like this, but it always made me feel special, and I wanted to be elegant just like her. She was a strikingly gorgeous woman with a Broadway smile and suffice it to say that her body—well, she maintained her dancer figure. She told me that she took her coffee black—no cream, no sugar. That's the way all of the dancers drank their coffee, she reminded me. She also proudly stated that, despite the fact that she drank lots of coffee, she had no idea how to make it.

Gretchen was indeed a mastermind because she coupled her knowledge of the media, the world of actors, and her drive for animal advocacy into the creation of an awards show, the Genesis Awards. The event honored members of the media that brought animal issues to the forefront in their productions. By the time I became part of the L.A. City family, the Genesis Awards had been going on annually for about seven years, and Gretchen had created a program equal to the Academy Awards, but honoring animals. I looked forward to the gala event each year I attended. It was a formal affair set at the Beverly Hilton—long dresses, tuxedos, exquisitely catered, and then there was Gretchen, the Master of Ceremony. As an actress and animal advocate, no one was better suited for this job, and I can only say that she was divine.

The entries' subject matter ranged from wildlife to zoos, from endangered species to factory farming, and everything in-between. Some of the film clips were difficult to watch, but all brought awareness to issues of animal protection. Just as Gretchen had planned, those that received awards were given extra traction in delivering their humane message to the public.

Despite the fact that producing the Genesis Awards was a full-time job, Gretchen was involved with and created many other animal-associated projects. She was passionate about L.A. City Animal Control because, when she began working in the animal welfare world when she lived on the East Coast, she managed an animal shelter. She attended L.A. City Commission meetings and presented her ideas for enhancing adoptions. One of the programs that she began at our city shelters was the Red Alert Program. The concept behind this program was that, if a member of the public showed interest in adopting an animal before the legal holding period had expired, then that animal would receive a red alert tag or band around the neck. This alert provided an additional security for that animal, to ensure that it was not mistakenly euthanized and to show that it had a forever-home waiting for it.

The tag was matched up with paperwork that identified the animal and contact information for the adopter. Gretchen worked tirelessly on this program, and when it launched at all six shelters, she made it quite a media event and invited her actor friends who supported the shelter like Alicia Silverstone. Not only did Gretchen's help increase adoptions and save animal lives, but she was utilizing the media to show the public that animal control was doing everything we could to increase adoptions and lower euthanasias.

Even though the Los Angeles Zoo was not part of animal control, I was well aware of the fact that Gretchen was a tireless advocate for a particular elephant kept at the zoo. She was relentless in her campaign for the transfer of this animal to a sanctuary, and after years of effort, she was ultimately successful. Again, my hero... She never gave up on what she believed in.

As I grew closer to Gretchen during my four years in Los Angeles, I would go by the Ark Trust offices to discuss programs like Red Alert or, truthfully, just to take a break, visit with Gretchen, and soak up some of her inspiration. I remember being greeted at the door by about five to seven dogs in a variety of sizes and breeds. Some belonged to Gretchen, some to the staff, and I think some just ended up there. On one particular day as I entered the office and was surrounded by the menagerie, a Doberman approached me, I was drawn to him, and I immediately cradled his head in my hands. I looked up at Gretchen and asked her if he had a neck or back problem. She just stood there and asked me how I could have seen that with the distraction of all of the other dogs greeting me at the door. It may not sound significant to anyone else, but I can still close my eyes and see the expression on her face at that moment. I felt she connected with me and knew we were alike because we were never "off duty." We were always sentinels for animals—their care, their protection...

Gretchen had been in the animal world for a long time, and I often wondered how she endured the tragedies that came along with animal advocacy. Before I left the city, she told me that she was getting tired and was considering retiring. She wanted to live in the country, get a Great Dane, and care for her horse. Selfishly, I didn't want her to go, but I knew she had earned this relaxed life with her chosen friends. Not soon after she retired, I learned that she had cancer and was undergoing chemotherapy. She died within a year of leaving the Ark Trust. I attended a special vigil and remembrance for Gretchen held in Los Angeles. Hundreds of her admirers attended...

There was a program for the event, and her staff created a mock-up of a Play Bill from Broadway with a glorious picture of her when she starred in "Hello Dolly." She was stunning then, when I knew her, and I am sure now in her new life. Even though my heart is still so heavy as I write this that I can barely breath because I miss my dear friend, I understand that she was needed somewhere else, and that is why she was taken away from all of us that loved her. To my dear friend, we all raise our glasses to you in celebration of all you have done for animals. I hope in your new life they are serving your coffee black...

Gretchen Wyler of the Ark Trust introduces actress Alicia Silverstone to Dr. Dena during a media event for the Red Alert Program she created for the shelters.

When I left the City of Los Angeles Department of Animal Control, Gretchen Wyler gave me this autographed photo with the following message, "To Dena, Oh how you will be missed. Thanks for your good work and your good heart!"

Chapter Nine: Exploitation of Dogs for Blood Sports and Dog Fighting

I would like to preface this chapter with a reminder that the experiences I am writing about occurred in the late 1990's when pet overpopulation and the number of dogs housed in animal control shelters were exorbitantly high. For the safety of the dogs, each pit bull had to be housed alone in a dog kennel after dogs were confiscated in a dog fighting investigation. This necessity drastically lowered the housing space available for other dogs. There weren't any independent organizations available to evaluate, attempt to re-condition, and/or provide safe placement for these dogs at the conclusion of each case as there are now. There also was no shortage of pit bulls in the shelter for those looking to adopt this breed—pit bulls that did not have the added liability of known fighting bloodlines. I ask readers to keep these facts in mind as they follow my experiences below concerning dog fighting and prosecution of those cases.

History/Background

As far back as the 12th Century, a popular form of entertainment termed "Baiting" consisted of matching fighting dogs in a ring with chained bulls or bears. This practice became illegal in England in 1835, but unfortunately, it was replaced by dog-on-dog combat. During the 1860's, dog fighting was outlawed in most states throughout the U.S. However, the brutal practice continued. Around 1940, dog fighting became an "underground" sport, and not until 1976 did it become illegal in every state. It still was not high on the list for law enforcement, and it didn't receive serious attention until court cases like serial killer, Jeffrey Dahmer, confirmed the link between past animal abuse/cruelty cases with future, progressive adult violence. In addition, many animal activist groups put pressure on law enforcement to pursue these cases.

I am sure that many of you have heard about dog fighting, that you have seen media coverage of fighting pit bulls confiscated from a remote location in your city or state, or that you have followed the high-profile case associated with pro-football quarterback, Michael Vick, and his fighting dogs. Many of these cases are discovered by animal control or humane officers. Animal law enforcement agencies with advanced investigative skills may conduct the initial surveillance at the location where the animals are held. Then they will notify police or the sheriff to partner with them on the actual "bust." Confiscating the animals and arresting those responsible for the animal cruelty is only the beginning. A cascade of events transpires for months or years as a result of the pursuit of these cases. The dogs are the primary victims, but a case also has far-reaching negative effects on the shelter, its employees, our legal system, and the public. Here is the rest of the untold story...

Often times, I hear people say that the reason pit bulls are used in dog fighting is because they have a mean disposition. The truth of the matter is that the breed is well known for its loyalty. That is an incredibly admirable quality. But it is put to bad use when a dog fighting trainer instructs a dog to continue fighting after it is exhausted, injured, or near death. Pit bulls used in professional dog fighting are specifically bred for aggression. Dog fighters will breed two aggressive dogs and cull any pup from the litter that does not show aggressive tendencies. They will then breed the most aggressive from that litter, then breed the most aggressive from the next litter, and so on, and so on. See the pattern? They have now produced the most aggressive dog from that blood line. There's a term in the dog fighting world that is used to gauge the quality of a fighting dog. The term encompasses not only the characteristics of aggression, strength, and agility, but also the eagerness to fight—hardcore until the end. This quality is termed "game."

As with any athlete, these dogs endure extensive training. A variety of training methods are used, and some include grueling treadmill workouts where dogs are forced to remain on the treadmill (harnessed) for extended periods of time in order to build endurance. Trainers may also use a device called a catmill or jenny (which resembles a small horse walker). Aggression and prey-drive have been bred into these dogs to a high degree, and some trainers will take advantage of this by placing a rabbit, cat, or small dog (bait animal) in a cage in front of the treadmill, or just ahead of the dog's position on the jenny, so that the pit will continue to walk or run for the duration of the training session, trying to reach and kill the small animal. It is not uncommon that the pit may be rewarded at the end of the session by actually being allowed to kill the small victim.

Another training device that dog fighters commonly use is called a springpole. The dogs hone their bite grip skills by athletically leaping into the air (improving leg muscle strength), then grabbing and maintaining their bite hold on a piece of hide or other object that is hanging from the heavy springpole. Their entire body weight remains suspended in mid-air solely through this bite grip, and as the trainer continually shakes the dog to try to disengage his grip, it acts to improve the animal's jaw strength. The dog receives a great deal of praise for biting, holding on, and not releasing his grip. This is exactly what a trainer asks of him when facing an opponent in the fighting ring.

It is not uncommon for dog fighters to hide behind the legal sport of Weight-Pulling Contests to justify why they own numerous pit bulls and have various pieces of strength training equipment in their possession. During these events, the dog competitors are harnessed to a sled piled with weight that they are instructed to drag. This, of course, builds their strength and endurance, which plays a crucial role in an actual dog fight because some matches may take hours to complete. I share with you a few of the basic elements of fight preparation to expose the degree of investment the dog fighters have in each of their dogs.

I recall a dog fighting case in the North Central shelter district where we impounded close to 30 dogs, including some pregnant bitches. It made sense to house the dogs at this location because it was the most modern and secure facility we had at the time. All of these dogs were originally housed outdoors on the criminal's property, tethered to their individual dog houses. They were never allowed to come in physical contact with each other because it would be a blood bath. So once they came to the shelter, they needed to be housed individually to ensure no contact in order to prevent injuries or even death.

This created a severe hardship on the animal shelter. The reality of housing these dogs was that we had thirty less kennels to house incoming strays and drastically lost flexibility to extend holding periods for adoptable dogs. So if daily stray intake continued at a baseline level, coupled with no substantial increase in adoptions, then the only shelter population management method remaining was euthanasia. The pits were held at the shelter until the case went to court, which could take six months to a year. So not only was it possible that euthanasia increased when the dogs initially were impounded at the shelter, to ensure a separate kennel for each dog, but every day they were held, it restricted available kennel space, and the euthanasia number began to rise exponentially.

I was warned by several of the Police Lieutenants that "friends" of the arrested dog fighters would probably try to steal these dogs from the North Central shelter. So we hired private security to patrol the perimeter of the facility in the evenings. Sure enough, I received a phone call in the middle of the night about two weeks into the holding period from the shelter night supervisor.

"Hey doc, just wanted to let you know we caught a couple of guys tonight trying to steal some of those pits from that dog fighting case."

"Are all of the dogs still accounted for?" I asked him.

"Yea, they must have been casing the place earlier and found out what area of the shelter we were keeping the dogs in because they came in through the ceiling and knew right where to be," the supervisor replied. "We caught them before they were able to take any of the dogs, and they were arrested."

I couldn't believe the lengths the dog fighters would go to in order to get these dogs back. But I guess it makes sense that they would take tremendous risk to retrieve these dogs when you consider the years of breeding they had invested in their blood lines and the money they could make by selling the soon-to-be-born "game" puppies.

About four weeks into the holding period for this particular case, one of the pregnant bitches gave birth to nine completely-adorable puppies. We set up a whelping area for her, and she was very comfortable in the shelter in her isolated area, nursing her puppies. It wasn't long until the word got out that the puppies were born, and many rescue groups not only requested to take them out of the shelter to care for them until the court case was completed, but these groups also pleaded that the puppies not be euthanized after the trial since they had not received any dog fighting training.

First of all, since we knew security was a top issue, we couldn't possibly release the puppies to anyone outside of the shelter while we were awaiting a trial date. Second of all, it was hard to explain to anyone that these innocent little puppies were probably not going to go up for adoption. I didn't even have the opportunity to discuss this with the rescuers because about five to six weeks after the puppies were born, we had to separate them because the most aggressive puppies were killing their littermates. This is a perfect example of why many of the dogs involved in dog fighting can't be adopted out to members of the public—no matter what their puppy-cuteness factor may be.

This brings us to the last complication, and probably the most controversial issue for the shelter, with these dog fighting cases. It is the final disposition of these animals at the conclusion of the case. If the prosecution is not successful, the dog owner will get the dogs back and find a way to engage in dog fighting again. If the prosecution is successful and the dog fighter is deemed guilty, part of the sentence may include instruction to euthanize the dogs, or it may leave the final disposition of the animals up to the agency that brought the case before the court. Not only is this a public relations nightmare for the shelters (especially when puppies or young dogs are involved that have not yet been in an actual dog fight), but the same shelter staff who have been caring for these animals must now go numb and assist with their euthanasia. As if the stress of day-to-day euthanasias of animals they have cared for during the stray holding period is not enough—now they must euthanize animals they have bonded to sometimes for over a year. This gives you an idea of the degree of post traumatic stress these employees must endure.

It is true that most of these fighting pits are very friendly to people, and there is a reason for this. When the dogs are actively involved in a fight, they must be handled by trainers and the referee in the ring during the event, and the person in the ring with them can't worry about being attacked by the dogs. This "people friendly" trait is misleading and creates another layer for the shelters to explain to people who don't understand how the animals' degree of "game" makes them a huge adoption liability. Even though they may not be aggressive to people, their drive to kill another animal is so high that, if a child or elderly person comes in between them and another dog, the fighting pit will do whatever is necessary (including inflicting varying degrees of injury/permanent damage to the person in their way) to get to that dog. The only acceptable adoption home situation would be where there are no other pets in the household, and the pit must be monitored 24:7 to ensure there is no opportunity to come into contact with any other animals.

The other risk is for the actual dog itself once it is adopted. Just consider how easy it would be for a dog fighter to break into the average home (less security than the animal shelter), steal these dogs, and put them right back into the cruel fighting world. Unless you have witnessed the horror of an actual dog fight, you can't possibly know the truth. I hope you will trust me when I say that euthanasia is by far the most humane alternative for these creatures. Personally, I don't think even the most qualified animal handler could guarantee the required isolation conditions for these dogs, plus take care of all security considerations for the duration of the animal's life. These are the details that make it next to impossible to safely adopt out a proven fighting dog into a home environment. I understand the frustration and anger that fuels the rescue-group and public outrage toward the decision to humanely euthanize fighting pits. (I can relate to it more than you will ever know.) I hope you can redirect this energy to supporting animal control in their efforts to identify dog fighting operations and removing animals from this tortured life. This inhumane situation is the sole creation of the dog fighter.

One final point on the large number of pit bulls housed at animal shelters across the country that are not impounded due to an association with a dog fighting operation... As you may realize, most of these dogs came into the shelter as strays in the 1990's, with no breeding or behavior history. It was unknown to staff whether these dogs have a history of dog fighting training or aggressive tendencies toward other animals or people. There is no argument that they are a very strong and dominant breed. Many of them are very friendly when evaluated at the shelter during their short stay, but this is what I have found. Some of you may understand this, some of you will disagree with me, but here it is.

From all I have seen at the shelters, all the dangerous dog incidents I have reviewed, and all of the dog fighting cases I have worked, it seems to me that this particular breed doesn't "show its true colors" of temperament until the dogs reach around two years of age. The stage of adolescence (less than two years old) is the most common age group you will find at the shelters. I believe it is difficult to predict how such an animal will ultimately behave and respond to potentially dangerous situations. I am not saying these animals shouldn't be adopted. I am saying we need to be fully aware of the possibility that circumstances may change once the animal becomes an adult. That means paying attention to warning signs. Many times when I did follow up on dangerous dog cases involving pits, where they inflicted severe bite wounds on people, the dog owner would often say in the animal's defense, "He bit a couple of people before this incident, but each time, it wasn't his fault."

Another common statement is, "He seemed to get more aggressive when he was no longer a puppy, even though nothing in his environment had changed."

These are examples of warning signs. Pit bull adoptions in animal shelters are delicate situations. One of the best things we can do is to make sure all pits are spayed or neutered as early as eight weeks of age prior to adoption.

I know this is a difficult chapter to read. What I am sharing with you is hard to hear, but I hope I have shed some light on the degree of complications for the animal shelter associated with prosecuting dog fighting cases. I wish I had more answers to make it easier for staff involved with these cases, well meaning adopters, and for the animal victims, but I do not. This is a true tragedy that requires our full attention and understanding for the safety of this breed and the public.

Dr. Dena holding one of the many, many pit bull puppies that could commonly be found at any of the six shelters in the city of Los Angeles.

Chapter Ten:
Pal the Pug

Throughout Los Angeles, there are a great many special interest animal activist groups. Many are breed-specific rescuers, some protect elephants and protest exhibitors like circuses, and others promote protection of Los Angeles indigenous wildlife like coyotes and mountain lions. Animal control works cooperatively with all of these groups and enforces laws balancing the protection of animals and public safety.

Within Los Angeles City Animal Control, we had officers that specialized in wildlife issues. Many had decades of experience in wildlife population statistics and habitat changes, and they studied the encroachment of people into these animals' diminishing environment. The issue of coyotes was always a contentious issue between activists who wanted the animals to remain in their natural habitat and the members of the community who encountered these animals and wanted them removed from their neighborhoods. As home owners continued to build their backyards closer and closer to the wildlife habitat, the number of confrontations between people, pets, and coyotes increased.

Some of these confrontations were just sightings that made people feel uneasy. Other incidents ranged from injury to death of small pets that were easy prey for these natural predators. In an effort to educate the public on how to coexist safely with nearby wildlife and warn them of the dangers, our animal control officers posted flyers in high traffic areas and conducted regular community educational seminars. Despite our best efforts, we received many calls of coyote attacks on small pets—cats and dogs that were dragged from their backyards by these predators. Some pet owners helplessly witnessed these events and were unable to stop the attack while others just reported missing pets.

The most prominent coyote-attack case that occurred while I worked with the city of L.A. involved Pal the Pug. What started out as a coyote attack became a twisted media fire storm of an animal abuse/cruelty case, and here is how it unfolded.

Lieutenant Folsom contacted me. He explained that he'd received a call regarding a possible animal abuse investigation in the Valley, and that he needed me to perform a necropsy (autopsy) on a deceased small Pug. He let me know that there was already "media buzz" about the inciting event and he thought it best if we had a neutral veterinarian outside of the department conduct the necropsy with me so we would have confirmation on the necropsy results. I suggested we use the Los Angeles County Public Health Veterinarian, Dr. Richards, who I had consulted on cases in the past. Lieutenant Folsom agreed he would be a good choice, so I contacted Dr. Richards who met me at the West Valley shelter the following day to perform the necropsy.

Dr. Richards was one of my favorite veterinary colleagues in Los Angeles. He was a mild-mannered, kind man and was extremely polite. He was of medium height and thin stature. His face bore some wrinkles that hinted at his age, but most who knew him for decades said he was a man that would never retire. He was highly competent and possessed a wealth of historical knowledge on every animal and public health statistic in Los Angeles. Lucky for me, he was eager to share all he knew with any interested young veterinarian. I for one was glad he continued his work; I had so much more to learn from him.

Dr. Richards arrived at the West Valley shelter and was waiting for me in the lobby. He was already in his field coveralls and was carrying a small tackle box which contained the special surgical instruments he regularly used when performing necropsies. Even though this was not a pleasant circumstance for our meeting, I always looked forward to working with him. Before we started the necropsy, I provided Dr. Richards the full background on the case as we walked back to the euthanasia room, the place set up for the procedure.

"This seemed like a straightforward case at first glance, but as we get more details from the pet owner, it is starting to unfold with contradictions and media attention," I told him.

"Not in L.A.?" he responded with a slight sarcastic smile.

So I proceeded to give him the facts as Lieutenant Folsom and his officers had collected them so far. "The pet owner claims the small Pug, whose name is 'Pal,' was out in their backyard two nights ago around 10:30 PM. The pet owner was indoors, but she heard a ruckus from the yard and a scream from Pal, so she ran outside. All she saw was the body of the Pug lying on his side in the grass next to the property perimeter fence with the skin from the nape of his neck to half way down his back removed like he had been skinned. She told our initial investigating officer that she thought she saw someone running away on the street side of the fence, but she couldn't identify anyone. She brought the dog inside and nursed it until the early hours of the morning while she waited for her veterinarian's office to open."

"She didn't take the dog to an emergency facility that night?" questioned Dr. Richards.

"Nope, she said she only trusted her vet—which I found a bit strange too," I added.

"The next morning, she took the dog that she said was barely alive to a vet located in the Valley, and he provided emergency stabilization care—administering fluids and cleaning the wounds. By evening, the little Pug had died at the veterinary hospital. The veterinarian performed a preliminary necropsy on the dog and came to the conclusion that a left-handed animal abuser had used an ice pick to stabilize the body (that's what he attested the puncture wounds around the neck were from) in order to remove the pelt with a knife but was interrupted in the process by the pet owner running out into the yard. The veterinarian immediately contacted the local humane society with his findings, who in turn jumped on the opportunity to put out a press release warning all pet owners in the neighborhood of an animal abuser on the loose."

Dr. Richards said, "You have to be kidding me with this story."

I continued. "The pet owner contacted Lieutenant Folsom because she wanted something done about catching the killer of her beloved pet and wasn't sure the vet had done everything possible to save Pal's life. The veterinarian agreed to turn over the body to animal control so we could perform a necropsy, but he wouldn't provide the department with his medical records on the animal.

"Lieutenant Folsom also sent out officers to the home of the pet owner where they looked for evidence on and around the property and interviewed neighbors to check if they had seen anything on the night of the incident. There was no indication that anyone had climbed over the fence near where the dog's body was found, and there were no foot prints around the street side of the fencing. None of the neighbors saw or even heard anything out of the ordinary on the night of the incident. Officers also interviewed the pet owner and found it difficult to get a consistent story from her regarding the timing of the attack and her reasons for not seeking immediate medical care for her pet.

"So here we are with a brutally-attacked little Pug surrounded by suspicious circumstances regarding the cause of death," I concluded.

Dr. Richards approached the small body on the stainless steel table. The Pug was positioned on his belly, exposing his back that had a large section of pelt missing. As Dr. Richards methodically began the procedure, I assisted and documented all of the findings. We recorded all of the general information on the dog such as breed, gender, color/markings, approximate age, and weight. Pal was a Pug, unneutered male, black and tan in color, about 3 years of age, weighing about 22 pounds. He had venipuncture marks on both front limbs indicating where catheters had been placed by the veterinary hospital to administer intravenous fluids.

Dr. Richards noted multiple puncture wounds on the left side of the face and around the neck near the initial location where the skin had been torn from Pal's back. Dr. Richards stated with confidence that these were definitely bite wounds, and I agreed with his findings. As he examined the edges of the wound where the skin was removed, he commented that they were not smooth as you would expect if the pelt was removed by a sharp object like a knife, but rough and uneven as if the pelt were torn or pulled—separating the skin from the body of the animal. He told me he had seen this exact presentation many, many times, and he had no doubt in his mind that the injuries were caused by a coyote attack.

"Maybe this private veterinarian has never seen this pattern of injury on an animal that has been attacked by a coyote?" Dr. Richards suggested.

"I don't know, but the left-handed killer is a far jump from a coyote attack," I responded.

Dr. Richards and I finished up the necropsy and placed the body in storage as evidence in the humane investigation. We walked back to the administrative buildings of the shelter to meet with Lieutenant Folsom and discuss our findings before I submitted our joint formal report.

Lieutenant Folsom was pleased with our findings because he had called it a coyote attack from the beginning. He said, "Now I have more concerns about the owner not obtaining immediate medical care for that animal as designated by the law. I want to get the medical records on this dog from the vet to see if he really provided treatment. I can't understand why he won't turn them over. Also, why did this vet make up this unbelievable story? We are missing something, and I am not finished with this case yet. I will contact him again to give him another opportunity to comply with my request or risk interfering with our investigation."

I knew what that meant. This incident was suddenly becoming more complicated.

The following day, prior to our investigation and necropsy report going public, I received a call from the humane society requesting to have their veterinarian also perform a necropsy on Pal the Pug. They wanted to assure citizens and their society donors that they were participating in and monitoring prominent animal abuse/cruelty cases that occurred in the city. Lieutenant Folsom and I discussed the request by the local humane society. We felt that full disclosure and cooperation with the agency, allowing them to also conduct an independent necropsy on Pal, would support our findings that the injuries were due to a coyote attack. This would be helpful in calming down the anxiety that had built up throughout the community.

We transported the body to the humane society and awaited their findings, hoping to conduct a joint press conference to assure the public there was not a pet killer on the loose and to educate them about coyote attacks and pet safety.

I was catching up on paperwork at my administrative office when the Assistant General Manager (AGM) appeared in my office doorway. I looked up and, before I could say anything, he spoke.

"You aren't going to believe this. The humane society just put out a press release confirming the results of the private vet that a left-handed dog killer is on the loose!"

I looked at him and said, "Nice try, but I'm not taking the bait."

"Dena, I'm not kidding. It looks like we don't know what we're talking about and that we don't care that a killer is out there," replied the AGM.

"That's ridiculous. Who's the vet they used to do the necropsy? I want a meeting with him," I responded.

"They videotaped the necropsy, and the vet is on record agreeing that a person skinned the dog. We should have known better than to trust the humane society. What a great opportunity for them to fund-raise," said the AGM, and he left my office.

I sat motionless in my chair for about fifteen seconds, and then I don't know how it happened, but the phone was up to my ear, and I apparently called Lieutenant Folsom because he kept saying hello on the other end of the line.

"Oh my god, Lieutenant, the humane society cut us off at the knees and are siding with the private vet's wacky report on the Pug case."

"You have got to be kidding me," replied Lieutenant Folsom. I never heard him swear or yell at anyone, but I thought this was a perfect time for him to break the mold, but instead there was silence.

"Well, now what?" I asked.

"I'm thinking," he replied. "We are going to follow through with our press conference. We will have all of our experts present— you and Dr. Richards. I want poster boards with details of the investigation on easels so we can walk the public through what happened and compare these injuries to those of other confirmed coyote attacks. But tomorrow, I am getting a search warrant for the vet's hospital, and I am getting those medical records since he refuses to give them to us and is impeding a criminal investigation. We can also see whatever other evidence he may have associated with our investigation. Are you on board?" he asked.

It actually wasn't a question because he knew the answer, but I responded, "Yes, of course. I will meet you at the shelter, and we can go together."

By 4:00 PM the following day, which happened to be a Friday, with search warrant in hand, Lieutenant Folsom and I and several officers were standing in front of the private veterinary hospital. The sign on the door indicated that the office closed early every Friday, by 1:00 PM, and that staff would return on Monday. I turned to Lieutenant Folsom and asked, "Now what?"

His answer was direct and simple. "We take the door down, because I am not waiting until Monday for someone to destroy those records."

I looked at him in shock. Was he serious? This was the first time (and probably the last time) that I tried to change his mind and convince him of another method for gaining access. I said, "If we break this door down, that means that security will be compromised all weekend, and I am sure they have controlled drugs in their pharmacy, and we don't know if they have animals in there. Couldn't we call a locksmith to help us get in?"

"That could take hours," he replied.

"I think we should take the high road on this. It will be worth the wait—less destructive, and no one will condemn us for being too aggressive, and we will still get in and be able to search for the records," I reasoned.

He hesitated for a moment and knew I was right. He called over to one of the field officers and ordered him to locate a locksmith and get him over there ASAP.

Within an hour and a half, we were in the vacated hospital, and the front door was still intact, but it had a new lock. The search warrant gave us access to the entire hospital, so Lieutenant Folsom split everyone up to cover different areas of the hospital. I started looking in recent medical files, trying to locate Pal's medical chart, and I went through files on the vet's desk, but there was nothing.

Lieutenant Folsom called me over to the reception desk. He was sitting in the desk chair rifling through the mail. "See all of these envelopes with return addresses from all over the country? These are donations to the doc and to the humane society to help them in their search for the dog killer."

I couldn't believe it. This was a ridiculous story from the start, and not only was it being perpetuated, but it was now bringing in money by pulling on the public's heart strings.

We all continued to work our way through each room of the hospital looking for any other evidence associated with the case, but we came up empty. Despite the fact that we saw other violations—like controlled substances not being properly secured and sanitation issues—that's not what we were there for. We left the way we entered, through the front door. Lieutenant Folsom was the last one out, and he locked the door behind him.

On Monday, we called a press conference. Lieutenant Folsom had it organized as he originally explained to me. He spoke about the department's meticulous investigation, stating that it did not produce any evidence that a person was involved in the attack. He had wildlife experts present maps of coyote sightings documented for the past ten years, maps that indicated the neighborhood in question to be in a high coyote traffic area. Dr. Richards presented the necropsy findings and correlated the animal's presentation to similar cases he had worked on over the past ten years. There was no factual evidence that the attack could have been anything else but a coyote attack.

The humane society continued to press the issue for the next week, and I am sure they continued to receive donations. Then something horrific, yet amazing happened. Lieutenant Folsom called me and said, "We have our second case."

I didn't know what he was talking about. Was there really a left-handed killer out there?

"A small white Poodle was just attacked and killed by a coyote in a neighborhood nearby to Pal the Pug. I have the body here at the shelter for you and Dr. Richards to do a necropsy on, but I have already taken a look. It sure looks to me exactly like that Pug. The clincher is that the entire attack was captured on surveillance video by the owner."

Sure enough, when Dr. Richards and I performed the necropsy, the findings in our report were almost identical to those of Pal the Pug. Similar puncture wounds around the neck and a peeling back of the pelt from the back of the neck...

You guessed it. We had a second press conference. This time, the media and the public were quite receptive to our findings. The humane society was conspicuously non-responsive and within days went back to their regular business. Their reputation was not affected. The public would rather have them err on the side of following up on a possible dog killer than to just dismiss the case.

As for us, no big "thank you's" for animal control, but we didn't need them. Lieutenant Folsom was very proud of all of our work and our professionalism.

A few details of interest that we learned after the case was closed and the public knew the truth—that Pal the Pug was attacked and killed by a coyote... During a deposition with the private veterinarian (as part of his attempt to sue the department), he was questioned about how he came to the conclusion that the dog was attacked by a left-handed man with a knife and ice pick. The veterinarian responded, "The angle of the cut skin led me to ascertain that the man was left-handed, and I knew it was an attack by a person and not a coyote because of the position of the stars that night." Soon after that deposition, the case was dropped against the department.

As for the humane society veterinarian that concurred with the ice pick and knife theory, I encountered him at an awards dinner months after the case had closed. A fellow veterinarian that was at my dinner table told me the vet I opposed in the Pug case was sitting a couple of tables over. He doesn't work full-time for the humane society, but does contract work for them every now and then, and he worked on that case. Before my husband could hold me down, I was out of my seat and making a bee-line for that table. I just had to know who this guy was and how he came to those conclusions about the attack on Pal the Pug.

As soon as I introduced myself to him, he seemed to recede back into his chair, and I told him I just had one question. "Why did you report that the Pug was attacked by a left-handed animal abuser?"

His response was unforgettable. "Because that's what everyone at the humane society told me happened."

At that moment, my husband caught up with me and politely excused me from the conversation. Oh, I wasn't speechless at that point. My husband got an earful of what I thought of that response.

I had learned so much in one investigation. But the greatest lesson of all was to stay true to the facts. Eventually they will take you home...

Chapter Eleven:
Tying Loose Ends Together

If you made it to this chapter, you are probably taking a deep breath and saying, "If this was your dream job, why did you leave after four years?"

Well, there are several parts to the answer. There is no one single "show-stopping" reason, but truthfully a combination of reasons that are similar to what each reader has probably experienced in his or her own career.

As I have explained throughout this book and illustrated through examples, animal control departments are highly emotional, activist-influenced, political departments. One issue or one position taken that triggers a negative response from the public can make or break the department's Director or General Manager (GM). The result is high turnover in these positions. The GM sets the tone for the department, so when this door is constantly revolving, it becomes very stressful for subordinate staff. It influences whether or not staff feel supported and appreciated, which eventually affects their work performance and the overall performance of the department.

I was fortunate that, for my first two and a half years with the department, the GM appointed to the position had moved up through the ranks as kennel worker, animal control officer, and shelter supervisor. He understood the sensitivity of the staff and the need for strong law enforcement in the community, and he was truly compassionate about the animals in our care. I had great respect for the GM, and the day-to-day shelter and field operations were running smoothly. As with all appointed positions in a government setting, you serve at the pleasure of the board or commission to which you report. When he was removed, it was traumatic for everyone, including me.

The human resource division began an employment search for a new GM which took close to 8 months. In the mean time, an interim-GM was appointed by the Mayor's office to manage the department until a permanent candidate was identified. The person selected for the interim job was a long-term City employee who had worked in a non-related department. She had zero experience in animal control or animal sheltering. Actually she had no animal background whatsoever and didn't even own a pet.

As a manager of my division, I tried to keep the troops optimistic and patient while waiting for the selection process of the permanent GM to be completed. The recruitment process could not be classified as speedy. As I said, Human Resources didn't start interviewing for the position for close to 8 months. Once staff found out the credentials of the interim-GM (by reading her diploma hanging on the wall in her office), they were not impressed. Her college degree was in home economics. Morale began to plummet.

Because the interim-GM was not knowledgeable on the issues of the department, she turned for guidance to one of the lead budget administrators (a long-term employee) who had connections with the Mayor's office. This woman was happy to advise the interim-GM and promote programs and her own personal agenda for the department. I had been close friends with the administrator for the past two years. We had both been supportive of each other, and not only did we have a great working relationship, she had also welcomed me into her family, and I enjoyed spending time with her kids. But things changed rapidly once the interim-GM made it clear that she was applying for the permanent position and needed the support of the Mayor's office. My friend no longer had the interest to maintain our friendship now that a new game was in town. I understood the situation and went about my work, but it certainly became tense at our downtown office among the top administrators.

The changes in executive staff were imminent. My dear friend, our Public Relations (PR) director, was the first in our close-knit group to transfer out of animal control to another department within the City. This was so disheartening to me. I don't think I ever really got over losing him, not only as a terrific PR director, but as a friend who made my difficult job so much easier to bear on those tough days.

Soon after his departure, a difficult situation was presented to me that sparked a huge divide between me, the budget administrator and the interim-GM. Here's what happened...

Several of our shelters had built-in spay/neuter clinics, and for most of my tenure, they were not in operation due to budgetary constraints. It was mandatory for every healthy animal adopted from the shelter to be spayed or neutered prior to placement with their new adopter. Because we didn't operate clinics at the shelter, we instituted a spay/neuter outsourcing program. This program was a collaboration with the local veterinary hospitals in each region to perform sterilization surgeries on adopted pets. Once an animal was adopted from a shelter, it was transported the next morning to our hospital partners for surgery. The system was working well, and it was a great partnership with the local veterinary community, but there was still a great deal of discussion from activists and Commissioners for the department about opening our in-shelter clinics and discontinuing our outsourcing program.

Because our budget was so tight year after year, the department couldn't afford to staff and operate the in-shelter clinics. The Commissioners decided that the most affordable option was to contract out this service. The lead budget administrator was assigned the task of developing the contract and handling the bidding process. After a period of time, an out-of-state contractor was selected by the budget administrator and approved by the City Council to begin spay/neuter procedures at the North Central shelter clinic and gradually expand service to other clinics at remaining shelters.

Prior to the clinic opening, an introductory meeting was scheduled with the contractor, the interim-GM, the assistant-GM, the budget administrator, and me. Even though the contractor would be performing veterinary medical procedures,

I had not been included in any part of the contract development or contractor selection. It was evident that the budget administrator had already developed a close relationship with the contractor, that she had provided most of the responses to questions asked about their qualifications and past history operating spay/neuter clinics, and that by doing so, she'd generated a great deal of praise for them.

As you may recall, the North Central Shelter (Chapter Four) was home to one of my top Senior Animal Care Attendants, Brea. Even though the clinic had not been in operation for years, Brea still did "walk-throughs" of the clinic to ensure that there were no maintenance issues, break-ins, or other problems. As I mentioned in Chapter Four, she was very thorough and took her responsibility for North Central very seriously. It will come as no surprise to you that, once the contractor moved into the clinic, Brea made herself known to the staff, offered assistance, and monitored the maintenance of the clinic.

Within a few months of the grand opening, I started to hear rumblings in the rescue community about issues with the clinic. Around this same time, Brea asked to meet with me. She presented me with a list of concerns— concerns about contract staff at the clinic not following policies and procedures, poor supervision by the out-of-town company owners, and inhumane procedures by the hired veterinarian. I knew I couldn't turn a blind eye to this situation because it was happening technically "under our roof" even though I was not responsible for the actual operation. Also, I knew Brea wouldn't stand for it at her shelter.

I knew that any stance against the contractor would be controversial, so I decided to write a confidential report to the assistant-GM (my direct supervisor) outlining the non-compliance issues. After submitting my report, I waited for several days to get his response. Prior to meeting with him to discuss the issues, I was confronted by the interim-GM in the administration building hallway. "Who do you think you are, leaking your report to the humane community about the contractor at the North Central shelter's spay/neuter clinic?" she snapped at me.

I responded, "Just hold on a second. I did my job and reported on concerns I had to my supervisor and no one else."

She made it very clear that she did not believe me.

"I can only tell you the truth, which is what I have done. Since I only gave the report to one person, did you ask the AGM if he shared my report with anyone?" I asked.

"No I haven't, but you can be sure I will. Now the Mayor's office is involved, and you are in a lot of trouble," she said with a slight smile.

Actually, I knew what was happening. I wasn't in trouble, but the budget administrator was supposed to be monitoring the contractor. This situation was an embarrassment for her and the interim-GM because there were complaints about the contractor from the rescue community and these complaints weren't being addressed.

The mystery of how the report landed in the hands of a humane group seemed to be solved when the assistant GM said he mistakenly placed the report in the recycle bin after reading it where anyone could have picked it up. I knew he was covering for me because he would not leave a confidential document where anyone could find it. The bottom line was that I didn't know how the report was leaked to the public.

Once the Mayor's office reviewed my report, a hearing was scheduled in front of the City Council to evaluate the spay/neuter clinic contractor. During the hearing, I was asked to testify and discuss the results of my report. I couldn't and wouldn't lie in favor of the contractor. I couldn't allow animals to be mistreated or the public to be misled. The contractor wasn't successful in proving to Council members that they could remedy the issues presented against them. At the conclusion of the hearing, the action taken by the Council was to terminate the contract.

Suffice it to say, I was never again in the good graces of either the interim-GM or the budget administrator. They not only blamed me for the removal of the contractor, but acted as if I had been disloyal to the department. It was not a pleasant environment.

Not until months after the contractor vacated the spay/neuter clinic at the North Central shelter did I find out how my report had been leaked to the public. Prior to submitting the report to the AGM, I needed to share my findings with the North Central Shelter Manager (the Lieutenant) because he was ultimately responsible for all activities at his location, and since we always worked closely together, I didn't want him to be blindsided by the report. I sat in his office while he read the report, and he agreed that it must be submitted to the AGM. I never left a copy of the report with him.

While I was in the Lieutenant's office and after he read my report, I was paged to the kennels to help with an injured animal. I left my personal items in the Lieutenant's office (as I always did when I did rounds at his shelter). When I finished my veterinary work, I returned to his office and took my notebooks with me to my administrative office. Nothing was missing, and I submitted my report to the AGM. Apparently, the Lieutenant had taken my report from my folder and faxed it to a woman associated with a humane group (she had been corresponding with him about issues with the clinic.) The report gave her the proof she needed to contact the Mayor's office and work to remove the contractor. I know this to be true because the Lieutenant eventually told me what he did.

"Doc, I knew I couldn't tell you what I was doing because I knew you wouldn't lie about sharing the report with the humane community. Sorry about taking the risk of getting you in trouble, but I was sure you could handle it. I would have stepped in if you needed help."

"What? Sure I could handle it?? "You used me!" I yelled at him.

"Look at it this way," the Lieutenant said. "By writing that report, you showed you were honest and not willing to cover up for the contractor. Good folks all know you always stand up for the care of the animals at our shelters.'

Initially I was furious with him, but I knew he wasn't attacking me. He had been around long enough to know that, if drastic action wasn't taken to get the attention of the Mayor's office, then the contractor would have remained in place for a long period of time, and the animals wouldn't have been cared for properly. In the long run, I was relieved the issue had come to a close, and I now knew how my report had been leaked to the humane community.

After the spay/neuter clinic contractor incident was resolved, some staff and rescue groups asked me to consider applying for the permanent GM position because they respected me for taking a position against the contractor in order to protect the animals. I thought about it and decided to apply for the position. I found myself competing with the interim-GM during the interview process. I was not surprised when I was walking by the budget administrator's office and overheard her speaking to an aide in the Mayor's office telling them that everyone was behind the interim-GM to get the permanent position. It ended up that neither of us got the position. Instead, they picked an outsider from a small humane society in Northern California. The interim-GM was transferred to yet another department within the city when our new GM moved in.

The new GM was a gentle man with a giddy sense of humor. He stepped into a job that was six times the size of the operation he was used to running. One of his mandates was to decrease the law enforcement persona of animal control in the community. This change not only applied to field officers, but also to staff within the shelters. Our strength had always been the consistent, high quality care we provided to the animals and our attention to public safety. We had been successful because our operations had a law enforcement foundation. The shelter managers were high ranking animal control officers, and the environment was very structured. For example, shelter staff wouldn't dream of walking in late for a shift or being out of uniform. Every detail of our policies and procedures were important and enforced, whether for the care of the animals, the safety of the employees, or our appearance to the public.

With this new mandate, I watched as staff attitude began to shift and the environment became more lax. Many managers became uncertain how to direct their staff, and soon this uncertainty reflected in the quality of our work. Our smooth sailing ship was starting to spring small leaks.

Tension in the field staff escalated as did upset due to recently damaged relationships between administrators (my friendship with the budget administrator in particular.) The new GM was very aware of the strained intra-department relationships, and in an attempt to unify us, he employed a wide variety of techniques. He hosted staff parties, visited all of the shelters in order to interact with the staff, and continually spoke on the importance of empathy. But he'd still been unable to establish a baseline of trust throughout the department, so he decided to try a new tactic.

To that end, I recall a day the new GM asked me to meet him in his office. I had no idea what issue he wanted to discuss with me. He started the conversation by congratulating me on being awarded American Humane Association's Shelter Veterinarian of the Year. He told me he was proud of me and that it was a great reflection on the department. I thought, okay, things are starting out okay... Then they took a bad turn.

He told me he had a special project for me. "How would you like to take the budget administrator down?" he asked with a slight smirk.

I was shocked at first, then completely insulted that he thought I would take joy in setting up an employee for termination. I knew he wanted to "clean house" and upgrade some employee attitudes, but I was not prepared for this. I responded, "First of all that is not in my job description, and I have no interest in this. If you want to get rid of her, I guess you will have to do it yourself."

He countered with, "But you could get even with her."

He must have done some checking up on the administrative politics and found out the budget administrator and I were no longer on good terms. I told him again I wasn't interested and respectfully excused myself from the meeting and left the room.

Everything was adding up to a department to which I could no longer give my heart and soul. I knew we'd had a great "run" together that had lasted four years. Just as important as achieving the goals you set for yourself in your job is recognizing when it's time to move on and seek out your next challenge. I was incredibly torn between leaving my "staff" family and staying on. I knew if I stayed, I would constantly have to be on the defensive—but this time, the attacks would be coming from within the department.

I had the opportunity to apply for a higher-level position as Director of San Diego County Animal Control, so I did. My parents lived in San Diego, and my husband and I spent a lot of time on the weekends driving to their home for barbecues, parties, and holidays. I thought that, since they were getting older, it would be better if I lived in the same city, so perhaps this job change would be the right move for me so I could be closer to them. Once I applied for the job, it seemed like the hiring process moved along very quickly, and in a short period of time, I was interviewing at the County Administrative building in San Diego. Soon after, I was hired as the Director.

Before I left the City of Los Angeles, I had a wonderful "send off" party hosted by my Los Angeles family. During the celebration, I took the time to publicly address each of my supervisory staff from all six shelters that were in attendance. I thanked them for all they had taught me and shared individual stories we had survived together. We all laughed, we all cried… but after the event, I felt we had closure and could all move on.

That same week, I was presented several Resolutions from members of the Los Angeles City Council in a formal ceremony. The female councilmember that made the public presentation thanking me for my contributions to the City over the past four years was someone I had worked with and for whom I had a great deal of respect. After the ceremony, we took the traditional photos standing together holding my plaques, and I remember she leaned in to me and whispered into my ear, "Maybe sometime in the near future, we will see a female veterinarian leading this department." She smiled, we hugged, and then we parted ways. I left the ceremony wondering if her premonition would ever come to fruition and I might return to my beloved Los Angeles.

Soon after, my husband and I sold our home in Belmont Shore in Long Beach and moved to San Diego. To this day, I still keep in touch with many of my former staff from Los Angeles. After all, we will always be family.

You may think I am being remiss by not including chapters in this book about the adventures that resulted from this career move. In two short years as Director of San Diego County Animal Control, I met an array of new characters from staff to animal activists. I limped through challenging politics, walked among elephants and zebras, watched the construction and arson of a new shelter campus, and had the final word in a large-scale dog fighting investigation. I look forward to sharing all of this and more with you.

Stay tuned as my memoirs continue......

Chapter Twelve: Photo Memories

Active Shelter Work

Dr. Dena doing kennel rounds at the West Valley Shelter... It was hard to resist comforting gentle souls while reviewing their cage cards.

Ill or injured animals are isolated from the main population, and their cases are reviewed and continually updated by the Registered Veterinary Technicians and Dr. Dena.

Vaccine Clinics

Pre-vaccine clinic preparation is hectic, but it's also a great time for bonding among staff.

This snapshot immediately prior to a Vaccine Clinic shows the collaborative effort it took to put together this event: animal care staff, veterinary medical staff, animal control officers, the public relations director, and volunteers.

Taking the time with people in the community, either in the field or in the shelter, was our key to success. We needed to show them every day that we cared for animals and that we wanted to share our knowledge with them.

Vaccine clinics allowed the Department the opportunity to interact with young children and educate them on the value of animals as well as humane care and handling techniques.

We also conducted basic physical examinations on pets at vaccine clinics and directed pet owners to local veterinary clinics for further care whenever necessary. In the background of this photo, animal control officers register residents for dog licenses.

Safety first whenever we handled animals... The Animal Care Technicians are expert animal handlers and well trained in humane restraint for the safety of the animals and pet owners.

Maria Martinez, the best animal handler in the state of California—over 15 years in the field and never been bitten! Pictured here with Dr. Dena...

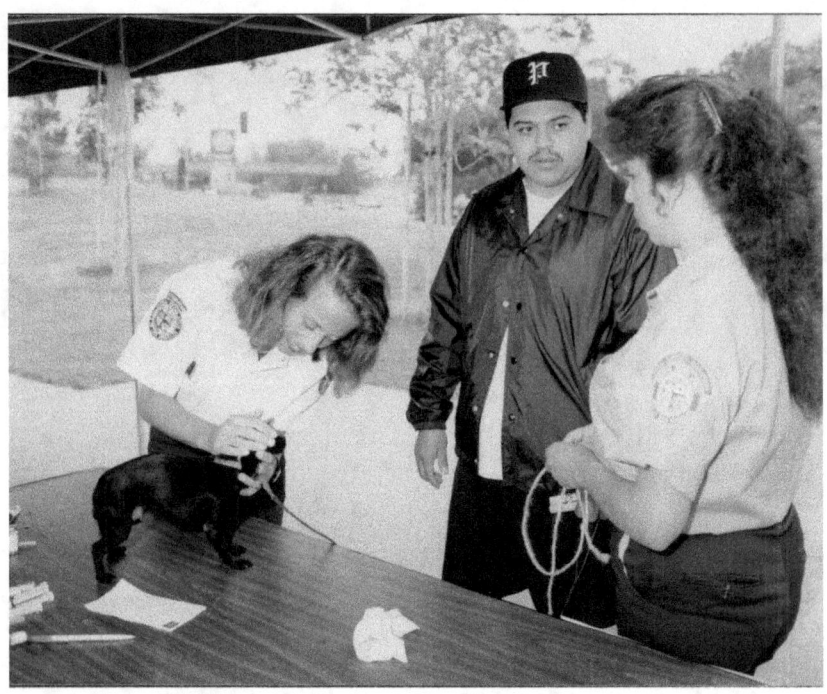

Dr. Dena partners with her ever-reliable North Central Shelter Animal Care Supervisor, Belen Castro, to work the vaccine tables for the little dogs. Sometimes they were our toughest customers!

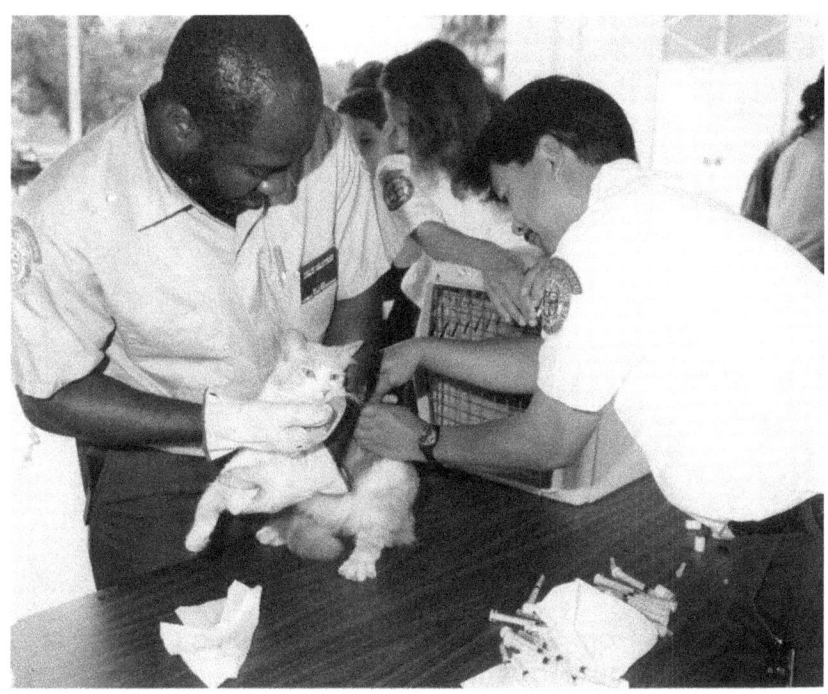

We also had quite a few cat customers in addition to the dogs. Registered Veterinary Technicians partnered with Animal Care Staff at the vaccine clinics. This photo features Ed from the West Valley Shelter, the RVT responsible for saving my adored friend, "Roody," that I adopted from Chatsworth.

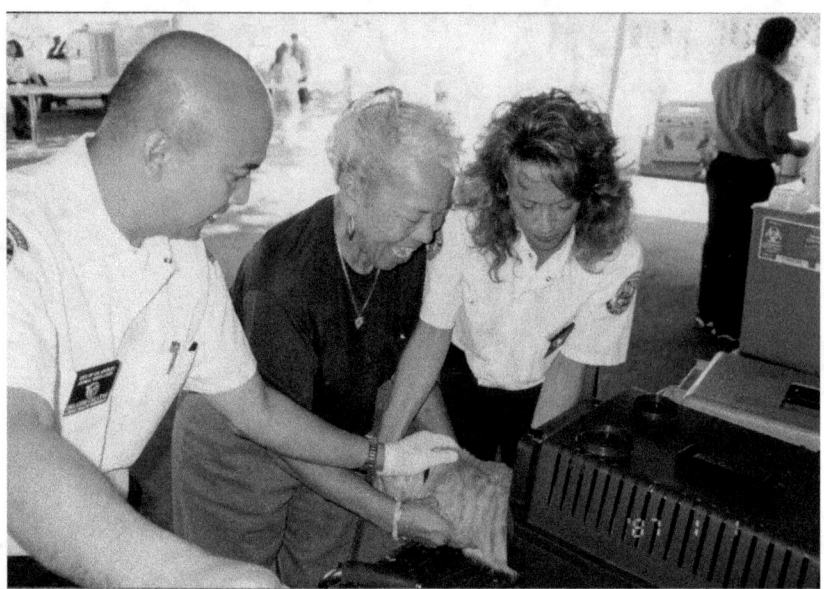

This woman from South Central Los Angeles brought in three healthy cats for annual vaccinations and was provided information on our Senior Citizen Spay/Neuter Program. Registered Veterinary Technicians from all six shelters volunteered to work at our Vaccine Clinics. Here is our beloved Orly, from the West Los Angeles Shelter—"That's all about it!"

Colleagues and Co-workers

Dr. Dena with her staff of Registered Veterinary Technicians
Back row from left to right: Ed Loria, Jeff, Rolando Villanova, Orlando Calayag, Richard Pusateri, Virgilio Tolentino, Ponn Thangarajah, and Marcial Evangilista
Front Row from left to right: Tony Ferrer, Janet Hudson, and Dr. Dena

Animal Care Technician staff at the East Valley Shelter pictured with the ACT Supervisor, Registered Veterinary Technician, and Dr. Dena.

Sergio Rios, Animal Care Technician Supervisor of the West Los Angeles Shelter with Dr. Dena, as featured in the Southern California Veterinary Medical Association (SCVMA) publication, *PULSE,* "Shelter From The Storm," February 1999.

The photo's caption reads, "Caring for the Animals: Dr. Mangiamele is able to examine this kitten's ears thanks to the assistance provided by Sergio Rios, Animal Care Technician Supervisor."

Animal Care Technician Supervisors, Registered Veterinary Technicians, and Dr. Dena, as featured in the Southern California Veterinary Medical Association publication, *PULSE*, "Shelter From The Storm," February 1999.

An associated caption reads, "Here's to the Troops: Dr. Mangiamele and Animal Regulation Staff look after the health and well-being of over 80,000 animals throughout the city of Los Angeles. Pictured here are: (Top row, left to right) Rolando Villaneuva, RVT, Virgilio Tolentino, RVT, Anthony Ferrer, RVT, Liliana Tossilini, RVT, Sergio Rios, ACT Supervisor; (Bottom row) Ponn Thangarajah, RVT, Susan Bullan, ACT Supervisor, Dena Mangiamele, DVM, Belen Castro, ACT Supervisor, Orlando Calayag, RVT, and Edmund Loria, RVT."

Photo Acknowledgements

Photos and all other content from *PULSE* appear by gracious permission of the Southern California Veterinary Medical Association.

Vaccine Clinic photos were taken by my brother, Guy Mangiamele, and appear with his permission. Employees of the City of Los Angeles Department of Animal Control agree to have their images used in publications related to the Animal Control Shelters and their activities.

Guy, an accomplished photographer, with his gear.

Newspaper Articles

In the mid-to-late 1990's, the *Los Angeles Times* printed several very-supportive articles publicizing the effects that staffing and budget cuts were having on shelter employees and animals alike. Some of these articles appear here, licensed from the *Los Angeles Times:*

Copyright © 1996. Los Angeles Times. Reprinted with permission.

"Vet Is an Army of 1" and "City's Animal Shelters Cut to Bare Bones," articles by Hugo Martin, featured in the *Los Angeles Times,* Valley Section, January 29, 1996.

Some excerpts—

- **Department That Impounded 74,000 Animals Has a Lone Doctor on the Job:** It wasn't a requirement of the job, but when Dena Mangiamele was hired as a veterinarian for the Los Angeles Animal Regulation Department, it helped that she is a former triathelete and an avid runner.

    As it turned out, she had to rely on her long-distance stamina when she became the only vet in a department that last year impounded 74,000 dogs, cats, goats, chickens, ducks, and a menagerie of other critters. The department normally keeps three vets on staff, but Mangiamele was forced to fend for herself after one vet died before she was hired last year and another retired soon after she got the job. A hiring freeze and delays in the civil-service hiring process have kept the city from replacing the two others.

- **Finances: Regulation and care services are big losers in funding squeeze. Fewer dogs, cats are impounded, but larger-percentage are euthanized.** Packs of feral dogs terrorize residents in South-Central and Pacoima, but over-worked animal control officers can only respond after a complaint is made or a person is attacked.

    Budget cuts have ended city-sponsored spay and neutering clinics; former clinic buildings have been converted to office space.

    Meanwhile, a lone veterinarian oversees patching up the 74,000 sick, injured, and neglected dogs, cats, and other animals abandoned each year to the streets of Los Angeles—50,000 of which will end up euthanized.

Welcome to the beleaguered Animal Regulation Department, the final refuge for the city's throwaway animals and the public's last line of defense against dangerous wildlife.

The department has suffered a 16% cut in its budget and a 29% reduction in field personnel since 1990. In the same period, the city's general budget increased by 3%.

Animal regulation is the only one of the public safety divisions—which includes the police, fire, and building and safety departments—to suffer five straight years of budget cuts.

Department officials and City Council members say the department is simply a victim of tough times. The city faces a $200-million budget deficit next year and is trying to respond to the public's demand for beefed-up police and fire services.

"It's one city department that is really in the most serious, tight financial straits," said Councilwoman Laura Chick, who heads the council's Public Safety Committee, the panel that oversees the department.

"I'd like to see it have more resources, but I can't raise [funding] much higher because what we have is going to the more immediate human needs," said Chick. Further hampering the department is its lack of political influence in getting a bigger slice of the budget.

Steve Afriat, a member of the Animal Regulation Commission, said the department has made some inroads to increase its budget but added that it is hard for his board to demand more when the city faces shortfalls.

"There just is no money," he said. "They are making trade-offs."

"Tails of Woe," article by Hugo Martin, featured in the *Los Angeles Times,* Metro Section, January 29, 1996.

Some excerpts—

> **While Packs of Dogs Prowl the Streets, Short-Staffed Department Limps Along.** [...] Because of [budget trade-offs,] the number of animals impounded at city shelters since 1990 has dropped 16%; there are fewer animal control officers to impound strays, and more spay and neuter efforts by private nonprofit groups, officials say.
>
> But in the same period, the percentage of animals put to death has increased about 4%, they say. Last year, that amounted to nearly 50,000 animals.
>
> "I can't even go into the cat room because I know they do not have a chance," said Gini Barrett, president of the Animal Regulation Commission.
>
> Shelter hours have been cut from six days a week to five, and medical technicians no longer staff the shelters at night.
>
> To pull the department out of its budget tailspin, department officials are considering a slew of revenue-generating programs, from a plan to license cats to contracting with private veterinarians and nonprofit groups to run spay and neuter clinics from the six city shelters.
>
> There's even a plan to charge pet owners $10 to insert microchips under the skin of pets as part of a new ID program. If a pet with a microchip turns up at a city shelter, the pet's owner can be identified simply by waving an electric scanner over the animal.

"Controlling Pet Population," in response to an article by Hugo Martin, featured in the *Los Angeles Times,* Letters to the Valley Edition, February 11, 1996, by Phyllis Daugherty.

Some excerpts—

> Re: "A Vet in Battle," Jan. 29. Hugo Martin has captured the plight of city animal control and especially of "Dr. Dena [Mangiamele]." However, the long days and crushing workload are pervasive in this tragically understaffed department. Dr. Dena is typical of the dedicated, professional management team being put together by new General Manager Gary Olsen to revive and revise the downtrodden agency. But no matter how good their plans to modernize methods and lower the euthanasia rate, nothing can be implemented without employees and decent facilities.
>
> Every caring person in this city can become part of an informal political action committee of animal lovers by contacting [your] council member and mayor and telling them you support efforts to fund and staff this department. We can also mandate enactment of measures that require owners to take greater responsibility for pets, including spaying and neutering. And we can join in formation of a nonprofit auxiliary foundation to fund such things as reserve officer and volunteer training programs, shelter renovation, wildlife education, humane investigation/enforcement, and especially breeding control. We must control the numbers or we will never stop or even gain on the problems.
> —Phyllis M. Daugherty, Los Angeles.

Van Nuys, "It May Really Help to Talk to the Animals," by Eric Rimbert, featured in the *Los Angeles Times.*

Some excerpts—

> An African gray parrot named Toto walks across a table and picks up a red block. "Red," he says.
>
> The parrot, performing for an audience at a demonstration, is also a teacher.
>
> Toto and nine other parrots are part of a new animal-assisted therapy program at the Berkley Convalescent Hospital in Van Nuys designed to help patients with memory and speech problems.
>
> The program, called A Bird in the Hand, is part of the Los Angeles Department of Animal Services Healing Power of Animals campaign. The campaign will compile information for hospitals, nursing homes, and individual health providers as well as people looking for a provider.
>
> "This project responds to an increasing number of calls made by people who want to know what the regulations are for starting and establishing animal-assisted therapy programs," said Becky Day-Swain, director of Volunteer Programs for Los Angeles Animal Services.
>
> Campaign chairwoman Dotti Bernhard said birds help people feel more comfortable about speaking and are able to help stimulate memory function.
>
> A patient asks the parrot to do a set of tasks, and by doing so, the person works on memory and speech skills.
>
> "The birds are less intimidating than a counselor or a therapist, so people are more willing to participate," Bernhard said.
>
> Several medical studies over the past decade have found that relationships between animals and people can translate into better health.

> One UCLA study found that one group of 65-year-olds with pets had fewer doctor contacts than another similarly aged group without pets.
>
> "Birds are very social creatures. They need a lot of interaction," Bernhard said.
>
> Qualified animal-assisted therapy programs looking to be included in the referral service may contact the Healing Power of Animals at (818)786-0020 or (310)841-0103.

Valleywide, "Animals Taken From Facility Need Homes," by Darrell Satzman, featured in the *Los Angeles Times*.

Some excerpts concerning events like those in Chapter Seven—

> Some of the more than 600 dogs and cats confiscated in July from an unlicensed animal rescue operation are now available for adoption, the city Department of Animal Services announced Monday.
>
> "We plan on holding all the animals as long as they are heatlhy and we have room for them," said department spokesman Peter Persic. "Some will make very nice pets."
>
> In July, authorities—citing filthy and inhumane conditions—removed 28 dogs and 589 cats from a Pets for Life facility located on a Van Nuys residential street. Doris Romeo, the operator of the nonprofit rescue operation that specialized in feral, abandoned, and diseased felines, was arrested and charged with cruelty and neglect.
>
> About 100 of the animals have been claimed by their owners while about 45% of the total, many of them already dying when they were removed, have been euthanized, said Persic.
>
> But hundreds of others, including more than 60 tame dogs and cats, have responded well to medical treatment and are ready for adoption, Persic said.

While healthy, many of the tame animals have been exposed to illnesses and have special health needs, Persic said, adding that the department will discuss those needs with potential owners.

Caring for the animals has cost the city more than $70,000.

"It's put a huge burden on the resources and staff of the department," Persic said. "Especially since so many of the animals are feral, their care and feeding is very difficult."

To inquire about adopting one of the animals, call or visit one of the three animal service centers where they are being housed:

— East Valley Animal Services Center, 13131 Sherman Way, North Hollywood, (818)756-8445.

— West Valley Animal Services Center, 20655 Plummer St., Chatsworth, (818)756-8485.

— North Central Animal Services Center, 3201 Lacy St., Lincoln Heights.

The centers are open from 8 A.M. to 5 P.M. Tuesdays through Saturdays.

Accolades, "Humanitarian Efforts Recognized by American Humane Association" from the *Journal of American Veterinary Medical Association,* Volume 214, No. 2, January 15, 1999. Dr. Dena Mangiamele receives the Shelter Veterinarian-of-the-Year Award.

Laura Chick (at left), Los Angeles City Councilmember, presents Dr. Dena with highest commendations to celebrate her service as Chief Veterinarian for the City of Los Angeles Department of Animal Control in April 1999.

About the Author

Dena Mangiamele, DVM, MPVM, MFS, is an animal shelter and forensic veterinarian. She received her degree in veterinary medicine from the Ohio State College of Veterinary Medicine. She earned her Master's in Preventive Veterinary Medicine from the University of California, Davis, College of Veterinary Medicine. She was selected as a Preventive Medicine Resident with the California Department of Health Services, Veterinary Public Health Unit. She received her Master's in Forensic Science from National University.

Prior to her shelter veterinary work, Dr. Mangiamele spent time in small animal practice and managing a nutrition and palatability care center for a national pet food company. In 1995, she became the Chief Veterinarian for the City of Los

Angeles Department of Animal Regulation. In 1998, she was awarded Shelter Veterinarian of the Year by the American Humane Association, and prior to her departure from Los Angeles to become the Director of San Diego County Animal Control, she received several Resolutions and Commendations by the Los Angeles City Council.

Dr. Mangiamele currently operates a veterinary consulting business, providing animal sheltering agencies with operational assessments, writing Manuals of Policy and Procedure, and providing expert witness testimony in animal cruelty investigations, with specialization in dog fighting cases across the country. She has also created a training division. This division provides classes for animal shelter employees on animal handling, medical care, and humane euthanasia. The division also provides classes for animal control officers and veterinary medical staff on conducting circus inspections and dog fighting investigations.

Dr. Dena is a vegan athlete with great interest in nutrition and fitness. She also has entrepreneurial experience gained through the creation of a vegan/raw snack company that successfully provided products to Whole Foods Markets. She lives in San Diego with her husband (also a veterinarian) and their dog and cat children. She continues to write about her veterinary and animal experiences in the hope of raising awareness about pet overpopulation and how the responsible behavior of every person can reduce animal cruelty and suffering.

About the Author's Family

Dr. Dena with Sonny, her Boston Terrier, tried and true friend all the way back to veterinary school.

Dr. Dena with her beloved Roody.

Roody with Dr. Dena's niece, Elena, standing next to the Christmas tree. If there were children around, Roody wanted to be near them.

Roody and Sonny growing old together in a forever friendship.

Dr. Dena with her husband Kevin (also a veterinarian) and their pets Roody and Sonny the Boston Terrier.